The Ministry of Reconciliation

The Ministry of Reconciliation

A Study of 2 Corinthians

French L. Arrington

BAKER BOOK HOUSE
Grand Rapids, Michigan 49506

227.307
A 776m

This book is dedicated to the Reverend Casey Forriest
Monsees, a faithful servant of Jesus Christ, who introduced me
to the message of reconciliation and who has had a lasting
influence on my life and ministry.

Contents

CONTENTS

Foreword

To a society characterized by fragmentation, estrangement, and alienation, the message of reconciliation comes as a rescuing hand to a drowning man. Every day in some way we are touched personally by a tragedy which cries for reconciliation—the debilitated individual, the broken home, the divided church, the warring nations.

The search is on for some formula that will pull things back together. Togetherness and wholeness are comforting concepts that seem to allude us today more than ever before.

But now again comes the trumpet sound of Scripture, "You can be whole! The breach can be repaired! The division can be healed! Reconciliation is possible!" It is not an exaggeration to say that this hopeful message of the Gospel could be the panacea for all the overwhelming personal and social problems of our day.

The biblical concept of reconciliation is nowhere more powerfully revealed than in Paul's second epistle to the church at Corinth. The thread is there in every chapter. The idea permeates the letter.

In *The Ministry of Reconciliation*, Dr. French Arrington pulls together those theme threads and expertly binds them into a strong cord. He shows the force of reconciliation in one's personal life, in relationship conflicts, in congregational disputes, in the sharing of resources, and in the defense of ministry. With the skilled insight of a scholar and the learned perception of an instructor, he unfolds in profound, yet simple terms, the mystery of how man may be reconciled to God, to others, and to himself.

Dr. Arrington's academic preparation and practical experience have prepared him well for the task he has undertaken in the writing of this volume. He holds the Ph.D. in biblical languages from St. Louis University and the

M. Div. in New Testament from Columbia Theological Seminary. In his present position as chairman of the Department of Bible and Theology at Lee College and as a faculty member at the Church of God School of Theology, he is known as a competent administrator, a respected scholar and a popular instructor.

In addition to his two other books, *Paul's Aeon Theology in I Corinthians* and *New Testament Exegesis*, Dr. Arrington also authored a popular companion volume, *Divine Order in the Church*, a topical commentary on 1 Corinthians.

Because this present work so deftly and ably draws from the Scripture such needed answers to contemporary problems, I believe it will take its place with the best of the modern New Testament commentaries on 2 Corinthians.

Robert E. Fisher, Ph.D.
Director of General Education

Preface

This book is an exposition of the Second Epistle to the Corinthians. In the epistle Paul reflected on his ministry and described it as "the ministry of reconciliation." *Reconciliation* is one of the most comprehensive words in the New Testament and is fundamental to all facets of Christian ministry. It touches the most significant issues of theology and life and is the very heartbeat and mission of the church. What I have attempted to do is to seek out Paul's profound understanding of the Christian ministry and to apply his inspired wisdom to contemporary needs.

The ministry of reconciliation has been given to those who have been reconciled to God through Jesus Christ. The fact is that this ministry belongs to the whole church, and all Christians are to be ministers of reconciliation since they are members of the body of Christ. The particular ministries in the church are part of this all-embracing ministry of reconciliation. No ministry is nobler than this ministry. It is to be practiced in the church as well as by the church in reaching people with the gospel and in responding to their needs.

The Ministry of Reconciliation is intended to be read and studied along with the scriptural text of 2 Corinthians. Hopefully, it will challenge the reader to reappraise his personal ministry and devotion to Jesus Christ. Paul has a way of exposing sham and artificiality in the church and of getting at the crux of the Christian experience. Over the years the study of Paul's thought has caused me both agony and joy, but it has never failed to be fruitful and edifying. If this book does not cause the reader some uneasiness as well as some satisfaction, then perhaps he has not read it perceptively or I have not written clearly.

It is a pleasure to express gratitude to my associates who have provided assistance in the preparation and the arrangement of the manuscript. Special appreciation is owed to my friend and esteemed colleague, Dr. Robert E. Fisher, who himself has a perceptive understanding of the biblical concept of reconciliation and who read the typescript and offered many valuable suggestions. His encouragement has meant much to me, as I have in the midst of pressures and demands of other duties persevered in bringing this work to completion. I wish to express my thanks to my longsuffering wife, Frances, for her assistance in proofreading the manuscript; to Miss JoAnne Sparks, my secretary, for her patience and skills in preparing the typescript; to Mrs. Debra Sikes Kincheloe for her assistance in research, and to Mr. Chris Thomas, a doctoral student in New Testament, for his assistance and encouragement.

French L. Arrington

1

The Ministry of Reconciliation

Emerging today is a new consciousness of the church as the people of God. This necessarily results in a new consciousness of the Christian ministry. The New Testament bears witness to the ministry of the people of God and leaves no doubt that their Christian service is tied up with Christ and His ministry. Christ began His mission in Judea and Galilee with the calling of disciples (John 1:35-51; Mark 1:14-20) and sent them out in His name to preach the kingdom and with authority to cast out demons (Mark 6:7,12). At Pentecost the disciples were empowered by His Spirit and sent forth as His representatives (Acts 2).

The apostle Paul was well aware of the close link between our Savior and the ministry granted to the people of God. He reminds us that the church is founded on the apostles and prophets, Christ being the chief cornerstone (Eph. 2:20), and that Christ has given to the Church the ministry of apostles, prophets, evangelists, and pastor-teachers.[1] Yet to the whole church the work of ministering has been committed and the work of those who exercise the special ministries (apostleship, prophecy, teaching, etc.) is equipping all the members of the church so that they might do the work of the ministry (Eph. 4:11-12).

---

[1]The Greek indicates that the "gift of ministry" of pastors and teachers is one and the same class of men.

13

The Christian ministry is rooted and grounded in the ministry of our Lord and the mission that He gave the church. Of great concern is a right perspective on the church and its mission within the plan of God. This may raise a variety of questions: Are God's ambitions and dreams for the church the same as ours? Could it be that the success of a denomination or a local church as seen by its leaders and members may be out of step with God's agenda for the church and the world? What place does the ministry of the church have in the accomplishment of God's purpose in the modern world where sin abounds and men are alienated from their Creator and from one another?

The greatest of all missionaries, the apostle Paul, must have faced similar concerns. On the road to Damascus he saw the light of the glory of God in the face of Jesus Christ (2 Cor. 4:6) and from that moment his heart was gripped by the ministry of Christ. In the course of furthering the gospel Paul knew struggles, hardships, hopes, joys, and disappointments; but he discerned clearly how the ministry of the church fits into the divine scheme of things. Nowhere in his letters is this more forcefully stated than in what is known as 2 Corinthians. This letter in which Paul defends and expounds his ministry was written in the middle of the first century to the church at Corinth, a church that he loved dearly.

A long period of time separates us from the Corinthian church, but what the apostle says to the Corinthians about his ministry offers much in the way of understanding the true ministry which God has committed to the church of the twentieth century. Paul's magnificent reflections upon the Christian ministry are timeless in their relevance.

At this point it is in order to consider a few introductory matters. These will set the stage for our study and exposition of Paul's grand conception of the ministry of the church set forth in 2 Corinthians.

I. PAUL AND CORINTH

Corinth was one of the famous cities of the first-century world. Paul, the apostle to the Gentiles, was the first Christian missionary to evangelize Corinth, which was located on a strip of land forming a land-bridge from north to south Greece. The city had been razed in 146 B.C. by the Roman general Lucius Mummius, but in 46-44 B.C. it was rebuilt for military reasons at the command of Julius Caesar and became the largest and most flourishing center in southern Greece. Along with its strategic military value, the city was wealthy and famous for its culture, its buildings (temples, law-courts, theatres), and its art treasures. No doubt it was the most important city in Greece in the time of Paul; it served as the capital of the Roman province of Achaia and was a great commercial and trading center.

The location of Corinth, on a main trading route, made it a natural stopping point for ocean-going ships. Sailors and merchants frequented the city. As might be expected, it had great notoriety for licentiousness, vice, and immorality. The lurid reputation of the city was known far and wide. Passages like 1 Corinthians 6:9-11 and 2 Corinthians 6:14—7:1 give us the moral atmosphere in which the Corinthians had lived before they came to faith in Jesus Christ. In Corinth, a city of about a half-million people and notorious for its low morals, Paul planted a church.

A. The Founding of the Church

While on his European mission Paul came to Corinth about 50 A.D. The Book of Acts tells us of this visit, during which the apostle founded the Corinthian church (Acts 18:1-18). He came to the city from Athens, where he had been only partially successful, but he met with a much better response at Corinth. There was a colony of Jews in the city, and it was in their synagogue that Paul first preached the gospel. In Corinth he met Aquila and Priscilla (Acts 18:2,3) who along with Silas and Timothy (2 Cor. 1:19), helped in the work.

Paul's evangelistic efforts aroused the opposition of the Jews (Acts 18:6-7). Because of this Paul found it necessary to withdraw from the synagogue and move in with Justus next door. During a stay of a year and a half Paul established a church there.[2] The majority of the church were Gentile, but a few of the members were from the Jewish community in Corinth. The fact that only a few of its members enjoyed a high social standing is clear in Paul's reminder: "Brothers, think of what you were when you were called. Not many of you were wise by human standards; not many were influential; not many were of noble birth" (1 Cor. 1:26).[3] So the Christians came from a variety of backgrounds, and many brought with them trappings and practices common to their lifestyles before they were converted to Christianity. The moral standards of many of these people were low. Some members were more affluent than others. Some members were intolerant of others, creating strife and divi-

---

[2] Acts 18:11 states that Paul remained in the city for eighteen months, but verse 18 of the same chapter reminds us that he "stayed on in Corinth for some time." If the "some time" is included in the eighteen months, then his entire stay in Corinth was a year and a half in length. Whether Luke intends to indicate that he was there longer than a year and a half is not clear.

[3] All quotations of Scripture are from the *New International Version* unless otherwise specified.

sions. There prevailed among them a misunderstanding of the Christian doctrine of the resurrection and the place of the gifts of the Spirit in public worship. All these factors created real problems. They disrupted the church, a fellowship so close that it can be compared to a body (1 Cor. 10:17; 12:12-17), and caused Paul great anguish and pain of heart. Everything considered, the congregation at Corinth gave the apostle more trouble than any of the churches that he founded. The blemishes and wrinkles of this congregation are abundantly exposed in the Corinthian letters.

B. Dealings with the Church

To the troubled church of God at Corinth the apostle wrote at least four letters. Of these only two have been preserved. Little is known about the two lost Corinthian letters, one referred to in 1 Corinthians 5:9, known as the "previous letter," and the other in 2 Corinthians 2:4 and 7:8, called the "stern letter."[4] Paul's first attempt to deal with the problem of immoral persons was not in what is known as 1 Corinthians. He had written a previous letter in which he warned the believers about mixing with people guilty of sexual irregularity, but his instructions in the letter had been misunderstood (1 Cor. 5:9-11).

The "stern letter" was probably written after 1 Corinthians but before 2 Corinthians. What the content of this letter was must be left to our own imaginations. However, he does say that he wrote with many tears and deep distress (2 Cor. 2:4) and that he had some regret for having written (2 Cor. 7:8). A church member could have stirred up the trouble by leading a revolt against the apostle (2 Cor. 2:5-8). Whatever the Corinthian circumstances were that prompted the apostle to write, his purpose was not to afflict upon them sorrow, but, on the contrary, to express the depth of his love for them. However, the "severe letter" did grieve the Corinthians, but their hurt was only temporary. The result of the letter was good, for it led them to repentance (2 Cor. 7:9).

The lost letters are of some interest.[5] What is important is that in the New Testament there are two letters from Paul to the Corinthians. These letters, 1

---

[4]The "stern letter" has also been referred to as the "sorrowful letter" or the "severe letter."

[5]Scripture refers to other letters which do not now exist. After the council at Jerusalem the church leaders wrote a letter to the churches outside of Palestine, informing them of their decisions (Acts 15:20-29). This letter, as well as the one the Corinthians wrote to Paul (1 Cor. 7:1), have not been preserved. So the fact that some of Paul's correspondence with Corinth is extinct is not unique. For some unknown reason God in His providence did not preserve two of the letters Paul wrote to Corinth.

and 2 Corinthians, record a great deal of what went on between the Corinthian church and Paul, and they provide the basis for our reconstruction of his dealings and correspondence with the Corinthian believers.

At the end of the eighteen-month stay in Corinth Paul sailed to Ephesus, where he left Aquila and Priscilla (Acts 18:18-22). Landing at Caesarea, he went to Jerusalem and traveled northward to Antioch. From there be began his third journey. At first he revisited the region of Galatia and Phrygia, strengthening all the Christians (Acts 18:23), and then he returned to Ephesus where he ministered for three years. Either shortly before or after reaching Ephesus, he wrote what is called the "previous letter," which seems to have dealt only with the problem of fornication (1 Cor. 5:9).

At Ephesus the apostle received firsthand reports of what the circumstances were at Corinth. Information of conditions among his converts reached him through the members of the household of Chloe (1 Cor. 1:11), a letter sent to him by the congregation (1 Cor. 7:1) and the arrival of Stephanas, Fortunatus and Achaicus (1 Cor. 16:17). Moreover, Apollos had returned to Ephesus from Corinth (1 Cor. 16:12) and could relate what he had seen in the congregation.

The news was not good, and this prompted Paul to send Timothy on a mission from Ephesus to Corinth (1 Cor. 4:17; 16:10), but apparently Timothy went first into Macedonia to minister (Acts 19:22). Shortly thereafter Paul wrote 1 Corinthians (about 55 A.D.), with the expectation that the letter would reach Corinth before Timothy and with the hope of correcting the problems that existed in the church.

The apostle continued his ministry in Ephesus while waiting to hear whether his letter had solved the difficulties at the church. Probably Timothy returned to Ephesus with a report that there had been little or no improvement of conditions at Corinth. Quarrels and factions persisted among believers at Corinth. Opposition to Paul's apostolic authority was strong. Aware that relations between him and the Corinthian church were going from bad to worse, he crossed over quickly to Corinth. He found distressing conditions there and his visit ended in something just a little short of disaster. Deeply hurt by the insults of the Corinthians he made up his mind not to make another visit until the state of affairs improved at the church (2 Cor. 2:1; 12:4, 21; 13:2).

After the "painful" visit he wrote what scholars refer to as the "severe letter." It was written "out of great distress and anguish of heart and with many tears" (2 Cor. 2:4; 7:8, 12), and was sent by Titus to Corinth.

The work at Ephesus was over. So the apostle departed for Troas where he expected to find Titus waiting with a report on conditions at Corinth. But his friend was not there, and the long days of anxiously looking for his arrival among the passengers on ships from Macedonia became unbearable. He could find no rest at all, being "...harassed at every turn—conflicts on the outside, fears within" (2 Cor. 7:5).

Still not knowing what was the outcome of Titus' visit to Corinth, Paul had no peace of mind. He decided to move on to Macedonia, hoping that he would meet his co-worker along the way (2 Cor. 2:12-13). This time he was not disappointed. Titus came to him with good news. A revival had broken out, and the majority of the Corinthians had shown warm affection for the apostle and deep sorrow at the pain which the church had caused him (2 Cor. 7:7). They were genuinely grieved by his "stern letter." Their sorrow had led them to repentance and had restored harmony and confidence between the Corinthians and the apostle.

The storm clouds had now cleared. Godly sorrow was productive of good works, and the majority of the Corinthians had become reconciled to their apostle. Out of gratitude for the outcome of Titus' visit Paul wrote what is commonly known as 2 Corinthians. Only a few months, perhaps six or seven, lapsed between the writing of this letter and 1 Corinthians. In the letter he was so thankful to God and reminded the Corinthian believers, "I am glad I can have complete confidence in you" (2 Cor. 7:16). He did not fail to admonish them to be liberal givers to the relief fund for the poor Christians in Jerusalem (2 Cor. 8, 9). Before closing the letter he warned them of the dangers of the few false teachers who had sneering contempt for Paul and who persisted in sowing seeds of bitterness that were devastating to the Christian fellowship (2 Cor. 10, 13).

Paul's controlling motive for writing 2 Corinthians was to prepare the readers for a third visit. When he revisited Corinth, he was afraid that he would find those who, in accepting the teaching and practices of a group of wandering preachers, had fallen into strife and envy. His desire was to promote and preserve the Corinthians' faithfulness to the gospel and the unity of their fellowship.

II. PAUL'S OPPONENTS AT CORINTH

Sometime after 1 Corinthians was written the opposition front shifted at Corinth. It seems that when 1 Corinthians was composed the troublemakers belonged to Corinth, but the opponents of 2 Corinthians had come from the outside. These people had no scruples about invading Paul's mission field. They worked only where others had already pioneered. They took credit for work done by Paul and boasted about the number of sheep they stole from him (2 Cor. 10:12-16). Previously they had invaded other Pauline churches. This is indicated by the fact that they were already acquainted with his letters, and they knew of the impression that he made on those who heard him preach. They said of Paul, "His letters are weighty and forceful, but in person he is unimpressive and his speaking amounts to nothing" (2 Cor. 10:10). These intruders were apparently in the minority, but they had defamed the apostle and had almost wrecked his work at Corinth.

The apostle gives us some information about these rival preachers who had wandered from congregation to congregation and had denied his authority while making great claims for themselves.

First, they were of the Jewish race. Paul singles out their Jewishness: "Are they Hebrews? So am I. Are they Israelites? So am I. Are they Abraham's descendants? So am I" (2 Cor. 11:22). Apparently they had identified themselves as Hebrews, Israelites, and the seed of Abraham. They were not native Corinthians, but must have been Jews from Jerusalem who intruded into the Corinthian church, seeking to undermine Paul's ministry and blend Christianity with Jewish and pagan religion. There is no indication whether they insisted on circumcision and observance of the Jewish food laws as necessary for salvation (cf. Gal. 2). These could have been planks in their platform since they claimed to be Jews and exalted both Moses and the law (2 Cor. 3:7-18); but the ultimate ground of Paul's gospel was Christ crucified and risen. The center of his faith and his life was no longer the law but Christ.

Second, the intruders considered themselves Christian missionaries. As Paul, they claimed to be apostles and ministers of Christ (2 Cor. 11:13, 15, 23) and to belong to Him (2 Cor. 10:7). The apostle charged them with proclaiming another Jesus and a different gospel (2 Cor. 11:4). They were given to self-commendation and boasting (2 Cor. 5:12; 10:12, 18; 11:18) and carried with them letters of recommendation (2 Cor. 3:1). These letters doubtless gained them welcome into more churches than the one at Corinth. As a preacher of the gospel, Paul boasted only of the Lord (10:15, 17). Over against his adversaries the apostle's humble behavior marked him as a true witness to the lordship of Christ. "For we do not preach ourselves," writes Paul, "but Jesus Christ as Lord, and ourselves your servants for Jesus' sake" (2 Cor. 4:5). His every thought was captive to the obedience of Christ (2 Cor. 10:5) and the power of Christ rested on him in his labors in behalf of Christ. This hints that the service and power of his opponents were not centered in Christ. They attached people to themselves and not to Christ and were dubbed by Paul as "false apostles" (2 Cor. 11:13). But with a bit of irony Paul found it appropriate to call them "super-apostles" (2 Cor. 11:5; 12:11b). They deemed themselves to be Christians and no doubt would cross land and sea to make a single convert, but Paul grouped them with unbelievers (2 Cor. 4:4).

More was involved than that they did not see eye to eye with Paul. Their faith was a veneer; their lifestyles inconsistent with the demands of the gospel (cf. 2 Cor. 12:21; 13:2). Their conduct and theology fitted very well the scale of values of the world. They commended themselves as Jewish Christians, but they were neither honest Jews nor honest Christians but deceptive unbelievers—servants of Satan, masquerading as apostles of Christ and as servants of righteousness (11:13-15).

III. THE APOSTLE AND HIS MINISTRY

In 2 Corinthians Paul bares his soul to his readers. No other letter from him

> sustains with such intensity the heights of the transcendental victory of grace in and through the everyday experience of the Christian believer in whatever circumstances, whether of exaltation or of affliction, he may find himself.[6]

The experience of Paul and his faith serve as guideposts to lead Christians into more fruitful Christian living and service. A look at two distinctive features of 2 Corinthians should refresh this in our minds.

A. Autobiographical

Of Paul's letters his personal traits come out most vividly in 2 Corinthians. Strachan's words remind us of this:

> The letter is an...autobiographical description of the ways in which Paul was accustomed to meet slander and calumny, physical danger and bodily suffering, disloyalty and ingratitude, from those for whom he had given of his best, the disillusionment and disappointment that invaded his spirit from time to time.[7]

Nowhere does the apostle reveal himself more as a real man than in his second letter to the Corinthians. He was a man of indomitable will and acute intellect,

---

[6]Philip E. Hughes, *The Second Epistle to the Corinthians*, (The New International Commentary on the New Testament), p. xvi.

[7]R.H. Strachan, *The Second Epistle of Paul to the Corinthians*, (Moffat New Testament Commentaries), p. xxix.

but he should not be regarded as a superman. He was very human. Augustine said that reading 2 Corinthians is like placing one's hand upon Paul's breast and feeling the very pulse of his heart.

The close personal relationship between the Corinthians and Paul emerges in the letter. He reminded them that he had spoken freely to them opening wide his heart and not withholding his affection (2 Cor. 6:11, 12). Second Corinthians opens a window into Paul's inner life revealing his desires, grievances and distressing experiences. Because of humiliating circumstances and trials "he had almost despaired of his life and seemed completely dejected; yet he had come to a new awareness of God's presence and power and was led to trust him more fully (2 Cor. 4:8-10)."[8] No doubt one of the church's greatest saints suffered and felt anguish like that of the lowliest saint. His humanity comes to the forefront often in this epistle.

> Here Paul is a minister of Christ, and a man among men; none the less so truly human because he was so spiritual. What hurt us hurt him; and nerves affected him, as they affect us. The whole Epistle pulsates with emotion.[9]

Despite all of his trials, Paul spoke of victory: "But thanks be to God, who always leads us in triumphal procession in Christ" (2:14). At times he was perplexed and almost despaired, but he declared over and over that the Christian has hope and that victory is inevitable. The firm assurance of the triumph of God's power is best summed up in Paul's own words:

> We are hard pressed on every side, but not crushed; perplexed, but not in despair; persecuted, but not abandoned; struck down, but not destroyed. We always carry around in our body the death of Jesus, so that the life of Jesus may also be revealed in our body. For we who are alive are always being given over to death for Jesus' sake, so that his life may be revealed in our mortal body (2 Cor. 4:8-11).

B. Pastoral

Paul's ministry was in two spheres. Most ministers preach to the home church or on the mission field. Paul did both. He preached to those who had never heard that Jesus saves, and he was a pastor who had to deal with practical issues in young churches. The sermons of Acts portray him as a missionary, but in his letters he is portrayed as a pastor.

---

[8]Ralph P. Martin, *New Testament Foundation: A Guide for Christian Students*, II, p. 184.
[9]Scroggie, *Know Your Bible*, II, pp. 140f.

Second Corinthians is the classic pastoral letter among Paul's writings. The letter was written to an unpromising church. The congregation at Corinth appeared to be one of the weakest missionary churches. It was in crisis, struggling to achieve a sense of identity as a Christian community. Though the Corinthians had caused Paul great anguish and had stirred up his ire, he was not a slave to his moods and emotions. He displayed the finest qualities of a pastor. He had no doubt that he was a minister, certified, commended by God Himself (2 Cor. 3:1-11). God worked through him (2 Cor. 5:18, 19) and his pastoral responsibility was one of preaching the gospel so that men would be reconciled to God and to one another. He refused to spend great energy on trivial matters and keep himself entangled in fruitless controversy. With trouble on every front he revealed the heart and character of his ministry, especially in one short statement: "...he has committed to us the ministry of reconciliation" (2 Cor. 5:19b).

It was Paul's responsibility to restore order in the disordered church at Corinth. In his handling of those circumstances let us see what "the care of all the churches" meant for him, and how it provides us with some of the finest examples of church administration and pastoral care. We see Paul as a pastor with fervent love for his people bearing the sorrows and problems to the Corinthians. We see him urging them to live out the implication of "living in Christ" and to practice the ministry of reconciliation that God has entrusted to the church as a whole and every one of its members.

IV. THE MINISTRY OF RECONCILIATION

The word *ministry* (*diakonia*) means "service" and is more often than not translated "ministry." So we read about the "ministry of the word" (Acts 6:4), the ministry Paul received from Christ (Acts 20:24), which was a minstry to the Gentiles (Rom. 11:13), different kinds of ministry (1 Cor. 12:5) and "the ministry that brought death" and "ministry of the Spirit" (2 Cor. 3:7-9).

The ministry of the church is its service, which is described by Paul simply and adequately as "the ministry of reconciliation" (2 Cor. 5:18). This ministry has been given by God to those who themselves have been reconciled to Him through Christ. To the whole church has been entrusted the ministry of reconciliation. Every Christian shares in Christ's own ministry or service and is, in this sense, a minister. There are different ministries as there are different gifts, but all the particular ministries are part of the ministry of reconciliation. This is an all embracing ministry—the ministry of all Christians to bring the healing life of God to a sick world of men and women alienated and estranged from their Creator and from one another. Crucial to an appreciation of the ministry committed to the church is an understanding of the term *reconciliation*.

A. Reconciliation—A Grace-Word

The Apostle Paul uses three grace-words to describe the way the gracious God delivers sinners from their sin through Jesus Christ. The first is *redemption* (*apolytrōsis*, Rom. 3:24; Col. 1:14) which comes from the slavemarket. It refers to the payment of the ransom or price that results in the emancipation of a slave. Man finds himself a slave to sin and death. What Christ did in his behalf paid the price for his release. The cost was beyond calculation, and it was nothing less than the precious blood of Christ (1 Peter 1:18, 19). A Christian does not belong to himself; he has been bought with a price and set free.

The second grace-word is *justification* (*dikaiōsis*, Rom. 3:24; 4:25; 5:1). This is a legal term derived from the law court. All men have sinned and stand guilty before God. How can a man be acquitted of his guilt and stand in a right relationship with God? The astonishing message of the gospel is that God justifies the ungodly (Rom. 4:5). By Christ's death on the cross it is now possible for God to pass the verdict of acquittal upon sinners; that is, they are declared innocent, as though they had never sinned. What made this possible was a mutual exchange: Christ took our sin so that we sinful men in Him might become the righteousness of God (2 Cor. 5:21). The Christian has been justified by God's grace, acquitted of his sin. It is a gift, totally undeserved.

The third word is *reconciliation* (*katallagē*, Rom. 5:10f.; 2 Cor. 5:18-20). Of the concepts used to explain the effects of the death of Christ, reconciliation belongs most clearly to the sphere of personal relationships. The cross is described in terms of two parties in court (justification) and in terms of commercial dealings (redemption), but reconciliation stresses the restoration of broken relationships and the response of person to person. There is no word more splendidly suited to express the goal and dimensions of grace, for it signifies precisely the reunion of the separated, the alienated, the broken.

A great deal is said today about reconciliation which focuses on either the patching up of a marriage on the verge of divorce, the mediating of a dispute between two factions, or the negotiation of a ceasefire between two warring nations. These have nothing essentially to do with grace, but in the New Testament reconciliation focuses on what our gracious God had done: "God was reconciling the world to himself in Christ" (2 Cor. 5:19). Reconciliation is a gift of grace from God through Jesus Christ and an invitation to a new and fulfilling relationship with God.

Why is reconciliation necessary? Adam's sin caused a rift. It disrupted the relationship between God and man. It alienated man from man. It smashed the whole history of man and the world. All creation got out of kilter. God attempts to mend His creation and to restore "men to their true relationship as children and friends of the heavenly Father and as brothers and friends of one another."[10] Men are divided into hostile camps "biting and devouring each other"(Gal. 5:15). Behind this strife is the hostility of men to their heavenly Father. To get rid of enmity toward God and the discord among men the dual barrier created by human sin had to be removed—God's wrath and man's hostility. God's solution was the cross (Rom. 5:10). By His Son's death guilt could be removed and the honor of God satisfied. Reconciliation is through Christ, that is, its ground is the accomplished fact of the cross.

B. Reconciliation—Three Stages

We can affirm three stages in the process of reconciliation. First, there is initiative from God. He, the Father of all mercy, acts to reconcile "the world to himself in Christ; not counting men's sins against them" (2 Cor. 5:19).[11] On His side God removes every barrier to the restoration of harmonious relationships and builds a bridge across the gulf between Himself and alienated men. God is the reconciler, instituting the whole scheme of reconciliation—making peace and restoring men to friendship with himself.

Second, there is the ministry of reconciliation. This ministry, committed to the whole church (2 Cor. 5:18), is exercised by the preaching of the gospel to the lost and by seeking to bring healing to people where they hurt and peace where there are tensions and dispute. The good news of what God has already done in Christ is the message of reconciliation. The proclaiming of this message is the business of all Christians. They are not only to call sinners to repentance so that they might confess their sins and receive God's forgiveness, but also to pray and care for all sorts of people—the poor, the down-and-outers, the drop-outs, the outcasts—so that they might be renewed by God's grace and triumph over their misery.

---

[10]Harold H. Ditmanson, *Grace in Experience and Theology*, p. 198.

[11]In 2 Corinthians "world" is understood in a personal sense to refer to all of mankind; this is made clear by "them" in 19b, referring back to "world." However, Paul does envision that ultimate and final reconciliation will include creation itself. (Col. 1:19-20; cf. Rom. 8:19-22).

Third, there is the acceptance of the message of reconciliation by us. The good news must be received. Otherwise we continue in our disobedience, and our relationship with God remains broken and our lives fragmented and pulled apart. On our side reconciliation is incomplete until we obey the command: "Be reconciled to God." It is not automatic, but the heavenly Father reaches out in love to us and welcomes us back into the family circle. Our responsibility is to receive it and make it our own. By opening our hearts to divine grace we enter into a new life of peace and fellowship with God and with one another.

C. Reconciliation—Its Central Place

The language of reconciliation does not dominate Scripture. Yet the idea is interwoven in all of the Word of God.[12] What is the whole thrust of the Bible but God's attempt to reconcile man and to mend His broken creation? His all-encompassing mission has been to reestablish relations distorted by sin, and, in particular to touch the lives of the sinners with His grace, dispel from their hearts the burden of hostility, and create a new people.

Reconciliation is an appropriate and important way of proclaiming the grace of God. The word is not found in the Old Testament, but it is expressive of what Israel experienced when delivered from the agony of Egyptian bondage. God made them His own people and sent them on a mission of reconciliation. But they failed Him, refusing to share with the nations His forgiving and transforming love.

Israel chose to bottle up the message rather than spread the good news of God's redeeming grace. They were preoccupied with their own personal concerns and concentrated on themselves. They did not communicate the reality of "reconciliation" to the world, but Jesus did. The forerunner of Christ was to make his ministry that of restoring broken relationships: "He will turn the hearts of the fathers to their children and the hearts of the children to their fathers" (Mal. 4:6). This anticipated our Lord's great ministry of reconciliation. He took the initiative to bind the heart of mankind to God. He gave Himself to the ministry of restoring the lonely, the broken, and the lost and bringing men and women into a close fellowship with God. His life and death was the means of reconciliation with God. It was through His Son that God did a work—a work unique and all-sufficient to bring man at one with Himself.

---

[12]The experience of reconciliation is variously described in the Old Testament (Exod. 3:7-8; Mic. 4:3-4; Isa. 11:6,8-9; Ps. 51:9-11).

Before the Cross, the Prodigal Son, the most loved of all the parables of Jesus, was the best picture of reconciling love (Luke 15:11-32). "There was," we are told, "a man who had two sons," and he lost both, one to a far off country and the other to Pharasaic self-righteousness. The younger son persuaded his father to give him his inheritance, and he squandered it in extravagant living. He found himself in a desperate and degrading condition of feeding pigs for a Gentile master. He recalled the comfort and security that he had once enjoyed but had foolishly forfeited. That boy did know that his father was waiting daily, longingly, and prayerfully for his return. He knew little about his father in terms of forgiveness and restoration. When he returned home, he found his father with open arms, willing to blot out the past. He had not ceased to love his son. In the house of his father the boy began to discover the joys and pleasures that he had vainly sought in a far off country.

The cross goes much deeper than the parable of the prodigal. Paul himself knew that the cross tells us what God did to restore prodigals to His heart. He accomplished reconciliation once and for all through Christ. It is complete and needs no supplement, but Christ has chosen to continue His ministry of reconciliation, through the power of the Holy Spirit, in the life and witness of the church. This ministry has been committed to believers and is now exercised by Christ through them. They are to proclaim reconciliation already accomplished by Christ, bringing it home to the hearts and minds of all people and urging them to accept its reality and power.

This ministry demands more than proclamation of what Christ has accomplished. It calls on every church and believer to reflect the style of life consistent with the experience of reconciliation in relationships with God and one another. At times strife, animosity and hostility penetrate the church itself and fray the fellowship of believers. Under such conditions Christians, still mortal men, are tempted to abandon the love that they had at first and the friendship that united them to God and to each other. No church is exempt from conflict. The way it is handled determines whether disagreements and frictions divide and wound the body of Christ or draw members together into a deepened understanding and commitment.

None of the churches established by Paul entirely escaped crippling conflict, but by God's grace he was a master at dealing with divisions within the body of Christ so that conciliation was promoted and integrity to the gospel was maintained. A prime example of this is his second letter to Corinth. The problems among the Corinthians had been heartbreaks; but when he learned in Macedonia that the people were repentant and were his friends again, he wrote 2 Corinthians. The first section deals with the ministry of reconciliation (chapters 1-7), the second with the ministry of giving (chapters 8, 9) and the final with schismatic intruders guilty of sowing discord in the Christian fellowship at Corinth.

Reconciliation is an underlying motif and fundamental concern of 2 Corinthians. Near the end of the letter Paul expressed fear that his next visit would encounter "quarreling, jealousy, outbursts of anger, factions, slander, gossip, arrogance and disorder" (2 Cor. 12:20). So his closing plea was: "...be of one mind, live in peace. And the God of love and peace will be with you" (2 Cor. 13:11).

The church exists to continue the ministry of reconciliation in its life and witness until the end of time. Countless men and women need to be brought back to peace and fulfillment of friendship and love. They need what is the heart of the Christian faith and experience—reconciliation. Its centrality is affirmed by Denney: "Just because the experience of reconciliation is the central and fundamental experience of the Christian religion, the doctrine of reconciliation is not so much one doctrine as the inspiration and focus of all...."[13]

---

[13]James Denney, *The Christian Doctrine of Reconciliation*, p. 6-7.

2

The Reconciled as Reconciler

2 Corinthians 1:1—2:11

W hat is a Christian? He is "a man in Christ" (12:2). This implies an inner transformation, a radical change that goes to the roots of man's being and makes him a new creation. He is reconciled to God through the cross. The healing touch of God has released in his life power to serve as a reconciler and to become a man of integrity.

Paul was such a person. He had come to understand that God, man, and sin met in the cross. Divine love that gripped his heart drew him into harmony with God and gave him power to become a healer of broken relationships. The defense that he offered to the Corinthians for his conduct—suffering, compassion, sincerity, plans for the future, and treatment of an offender—bears witness that he was a man of honesty and was devoted to the ministry of reconciliation.

I. GRACE AND PEACE (1:1-2)

Paul's ministry had been challenged by the false apostles. They invaded the church at Corinth and sought to undermine his authority (chapters 10-13). To counter their aspersions he made a special point of describing himself as an apostle, one called and sent forth by God to preach the gospel. This is the essential qualification of a preacher. "How can they preach unless they are sent?" (Rom. 10:15). The apostle was conscious that his message of grace *(charis)* and peace *(eirēnē)* could meet the needs of men in their spiritual hunger, their purposeless living, their feeling of being crushed by harsh experiences in life and their sense of living in hell on earth.

The apostle had preached this message to the Corinthians on his first visit to their city. A number of them received the gospel, but in the opening of 2 Corinthians he prayed they would abound more fully in grace and peace.

Grace is God's redeeming favor toward the undeserving. It awakens repentance and faith in us and restores us to fellowship with God. Grace suggests power, but not as something distinct from Christ Himself. Paul prayed for the removal of a thorn in the flesh. Christ reminded him: "My grace is sufficient for you, for my power is made perfect in weakness" (12:9). Grace comes in the person of Jesus Christ and is His active presence for the salvation of men.

Peace, sadly needed in the Corinthian church, is the fruit of God's saving grace. The mission of Jesus was described as preaching peace to all men, near and far (Eph. 2:17). A popular notion of peace is the absence of trouble, but in the biblical sense the term refers to wholeness, harmony, health, well-being. As opposed to chaos and disunity, a modern equivalent is "integration." Peace is "spiritual wholeness" which produces a harmonious and fulfilling fellowship with others. Such peace comes only to those of us who have been made one in Jesus Christ through our reconciliation with God. This peace, however, should not be thought of as necessarily trouble-free. Those in harmony with God are to continue to resist temptations in themselves and to struggle against evil in the world.

There are two distinct elements in peace. First, its basis is reconciliation with God, the result of His restoring grace. Bitter antagonism and resentment toward God are rooted in our self-will. When we see sin for what it is and are led to repentance, God's forgiving love restores us to friendship with Him. Our hostility is overcome and Christ becomes our peace—"Peace with God through our Lord Jesus Christ" (Rom. 5:1).

Second, peace must be basic to human relations. There can be no complete peace until we are reconciled to one another. Jesus gave this high priority in His teaching. He reminds us that if a brother has a grievance against us, our duty is to seek his reconciliation (Matt. 5:23-24). There is no shift in responsibility, even if it is the brother who is at fault and has done the injury.

God is the ultimate healer of rifts among Christians. No one knew better than Paul that the gaining and maintaining of unity requires divine help. So he prayed for the Corinthians to have a deeper experience of grace and peace, both of which have their center and source in God the Father and Christ the Son.

II. PERSONAL COMPASSION AND COMFORT (1:3-11)

As a servant of Christ Paul had experienced suffering and troubles. Almost instinctively he sounded a note of thanks to God for comfort given him: "Praise be to God and Father of our Lord Jesus Christ."

A. The Source of Compassion and Comfort (1:3-4).

The fact that God delivers the afflicted and oppressed led Paul to bless Him. The apostle had found Him to be "the Father of compassion and the God of all comfort." The key word is comfort (*paraklēsis*). It occurs ten times in verses 3-5. The Greek verb form basically means "to appeal," "to exhort," "to encourage." Comfort, then, is an urging, a compelling, an encouragement which strengthens and consoles the sufferer. Christians know that God is the only source of encouragement and strength.

The divine strength that Paul had received in the face of crises and in deliverance from affliction made him more conscious of God's love. The continued comfort granted to Paul was not merely for his own benefit; it was given so that he could console others in need of comfort. The hurts and the agonies (7:6; 11:23-27) in which he found the comfort of God prepared him to give the same comfort to others. His ministry of comforting was not through the radiance and the strength of his personality but through the comfort of God, which was his equipment for service. God allowed him to share in the harsh realities of life. His sufferings enabled him to come alongside those in similar circumstances and feel their pain. He had sat where they sat. Our suffering, too, has a place in the purpose of God.

B. The Interchange of Suffering and Comfort (1:5-7)

The sufferings of Christ overflowed into the church. Paul did not speak of his sufferings as his own but as the sufferings of Christ. These reached him in fellowship and service of Christ (4:8-12; 6:4-10) and are to be endured in some measure by all Christians. Of course Christ's suffering and death were unique and all-sufficient to break through the barrier of sin between God and us.

On the cross he bore our guilt. "God made him who had no sin to be sin for us, so that in him we might become the righteousness of God" (5:21). In this sense no one can share in the sufferings of Christ. His mighty work of reconciliation is an accomplished fact. It is complete and needs no supplement. However, the same Jesus called his followers to take up the cross and follow Him. To obey is to enter into the fellowship of His suffering.

No one can add any saving value to Christ's sufferings, but Paul's participation in them was not futile. Great troubles were endured by him for the spiritual benefit of the Corinthians. There was an interchange: the suffering of Paul became comfort to the Corinthians. God blessed him in his sufferings so that he could better serve the believers at Corinth. He paid the cost to bring them the gospel and to comfort them in trials, but they, too, would have to endure the same sufferings because they were followers of Christ.

Suffering and comfort, common to the life of Christians, are not a matter of bad and good fortune but are permitted by God for the specific purpose of blessing. Confident of this Paul reminded the Corinthians, "Our hope for you is firm, because we know that just as you share in our sufferings, so also you share in our comfort." Divine comfort that abounded through Paul worked for their deliverance from sin and death. Such comfort produced in them patient endurance as they shared in the sufferings of Christ.[1] As in the case of the Corinthians, the Christian finds that suffering and comfort go together. Whatever trials and afflictions the Christian shares with Christ are more than counter balanced by strength and comfort received from above.

C. The Peril in Asia (1:8-11)

Now the apostle recalled a recent deliverance from a crushing experience. His desire was not to conceal his tribulations. For him they were not tokens of failure and defeat, but a source of encouragement for the Corinthians. He did not bother to give them any details of the event. The dangerous affliction did occur in the Roman province of Asia. Its chief city was Ephesus.

The apostle had had trouble in Ephesus, but the riot of Acts 19:23-40 in the city does not seem to have been so grave as to bring him to death's door. Very likely it was the kind of danger that he speaks of in 11:23-26, where he reminds us that he had been exposed to death again and again.

Whatever the exact nature of the peril, the result was despair. He was like a ship that is overloaded with cargo and is gradually sinking. His burden was too

---

[1] 1 Peter 2:19-23 makes it clear that being buffeted for our doing wrong is another matter.

great. His condition, so he thought, was fatal. Convinced "the sentence of death"[2] had been passed on him, he gave up all hope of living. He lost confidence in anything he could do. Death knocked on his door, but his suffering was not futile. What happened threw him back on God and his mercy. The adversity and deliverance taught him not to rely on himself but on God who raises the dead.

True comfort and security are always in God's hands. The threat of death reminds us of the limits of all human comfort and security. Our only hope lies in the resurrection of the dead. Where resurrection takes place, God and God alone is at work. God is the master of both life and death, as Christ's death and resurrection have made clear.

God rescued Paul in a dangerous situation. He learned the hard way the vanity of self-confidence and the importance of confidence in God. Like most of us he did not know what the future held, but he knew the One who holds the future. Grave perils and dangers would come again; but none of these, including death, was his worry. Regardless of their gravity, he assured the Christians at Corinth that he would not despair. "On him we have set our hope that he will continue to deliver us, as you help us by your prayers." He believed in the prayer of God's people and expected the church to minister in future crises by praying for him. When God answered their prayers on his behalf, this would lead many others to give thanks for God's "gracious favor" (*charisma*, a gift of grace)[3] toward Paul.

III. PERSONAL SINCERITY (1:12-14)

Good human relations depend on mutual confidence, but Paul's spiritual children at Corinth accused him of base motives.[4] It appeared to them that he was insincere and fickle, promising one thing, but doing another when convenience or self-interest so dictated. In dealing with that charge Paul, in the interest of understanding and reconciliation, offered a twofold defense.

---

[2]"The sentence of death" (*apokrima*) is ambiguous. It probably indicates that Paul felt like a prisoner who had asked for mercy but had been told that he must die.

[3]*Charisma* has many meanings, but here the context indicates that the word refers primarily to an act of deliverance. God granted His favor to Paul in rescuing him from death.

[4]The accusations of the Corinthians are implied in what is stated in 1:12-14.

A. Attested by His Pure Motives and Conduct (1:12)

Only in "holiness and sincerity," that is, in honesty prompted by God had he conducted himself. Amid all the anxieties and distresses he had an inner consolation. His conscience bore witness that he had never deceived anyone. His ministry and conduct throughout the world and especially at Corinth were marked by sincerity. Special care had been taken in his dealings with the Corinthians. He declined to take pay from them, but he could say, "I robbed other churches by receiving support from them so as to serve you" (11:8).

No doubt there were good reasons for caution in his relations with that church. What he did as a minister was not "according to worldly wisdom." That is, he was not a clever double-dealer, prompted by motives of self-seeking, doing only what was in his interest. On the contrary, he was guided by the grace of God. Nothing but grace (*charis*) reconciled Paul to God and equipped him for ministry. The continuance of divine favor enabled him to persist in the Christian life and fulfill the ministry entrusted to him. The thought of God's condescending love for him and all mankind in the reconciling work of Christ was what controlled his life. Holiness and grace, marked his dealings with the Corinthians. These were fruit of God's grace.

B. Attested by His Letters (1:13-14)

Sincerity marked the life of Paul. In his letters he had no desire to mislead or to create misunderstanding. What he wrote was straightforward, but he had been charged with deliberately writing obscure and deceptive letters. He had stated exactly what he wished to say. They did not need to read between the lines.

The Corinthians did not know the apostle very well. Otherwise they would have affirmed his sincerity rather than suspecting him of bad motives. God's grace through Paul was responsible for their faith. A fuller understanding of their apostle would make them appreciate what God's grace continued to do through him. Though they did not know him very well yet, he desired that they come to discern his sincerity and what his letters meant. Should they fully understand him, they could take pride in him as he would in them in the day of judgment.

On that day Christ will disclose all hidden secrets (5:10; 1 Cor. 4:5). All who have loved each other and have promoted fellowship among God's people will rejoice. But there will be no joy for those who have destroyed the reputation of others or have set Christians at odds with one another by charges of insincerity.

IV. POSTPONEMENT OF A PROPOSED VISIT
(1:15—2:4)

Plans had been made by Paul to visit Corinth, but circumstances forced him to wait a while. This gave rise to misunderstanding among the Corinthians. So he tried to reconcile them to the change of plans.

A. His Original Travel Plans (1:15-16)

At first he intended to go from Ephesus to Corinth, on northward to Macedonia, back to Corinth and on to Judea. Perhaps in the "stern letter" he told them that he would visit them twice in the near future. He changed his mind upon hearing of the crises in the Corinthian church. There was nothing wrong with his change of travel plans, but his enemies in Corinth seized it as an opportunity to accuse him of indecision and of neglecting the church.[5]

He did not hesitate in answering the charges. Personal criticism was not feared by him as a "no-no." He was able to handle it fairly and openly. The need for unity took high priority in his thinking. "Live in harmony with one another" (Rom. 12:16). "If it is possible, as far as it depends on you, live at peace with everyone" (Rom. 12:18). "Let us therefore make every effort to do what leads to peace" (Rom. 14:19). "Live in peace with each other" (I Thess. 5:13).

Yet Paul, a strong advocate of peace, found himself involved in personal and church disputes (Gal. 2:11-14; Acts 15:1-2, 36-40). This does not change the fact that he was a reconciling person. He communicated acceptance and understanding so as to break down walls of hostility. To those who mistrusted and misunderstood him he constructed bridges of communication and trust.

Above all he knew the establishment and maintenance of trust-relationships were vital if true reconciliation was to take place. This reflected the way he dealt with the grievances of the Corinthians. He was willing to meet them in the arena of trust and open up his heart to them. Misunderstandings and hurt feelings carry the potential for destructive bitterness. It is wise for Christians to resolve frictions so that trust is re-established and the church can move on for the glory of God. We have a good example in Paul's explanation to the Corinthian converts that his change of plans was in good faith.

---

[5]In 1:15-16 Paul does not specifically state what the charges were, but from what he said it is clear that they had accused him of irresponsibility.

B. His New Travel Plans (1:17-22)

Apparently Paul had planned to visit Corinth twice during his Macedonian ministry (1:16; 1 Cor. 16:5-8), but he canceled his visits of which he had given them notice. Because of troubles in the church he decided not to make a journey at that time to Corinth. The shift of plans had led to two charges: (1) He was vacillating and irresponsible, taking the affairs of the church lightly. (2) He made his plans according to merely human standards and changed them to fit his own interest. His word was no more reliable, so they said, than the double-talk of a worldly man who answered Yes and No in the same breath. Paul's response to the charges lifted the whole matter to the highest level.

1. The promises of God. (1:19-20). The apostle was more interested in defending the gospel than himself. The truth was that the Corinthians' charge that he had not been honest and open in his dealings with them reflected not only on him but also cast a shadow across his message. In response Paul pointed to the faithfulness of God. His word was unfailing. What God had promised He had done. In Corinth the apostle and his co-workers, Silas and Timothy, had preached that Jesus is Lord. Through Him God faithfully fulfilled the promises announced in the Old Testament. "For no matter how many promises God has made, they are 'yes' in Christ." When Christians in worship uttered "Amen" ("So be it"), they said Yes to Christ and thereby confessed that they believed that He affirmed all God's promises.

The great promises of God are as numerous in the Old Testament as stars in the sky on a clear night. They unfold His purpose, first declared to Abraham, that from him would spring a nation through which God would reveal Himself to all men (Gen. 12:1-3). Foremost among them was the promise of forgiving mercy that would restore men to fellowship with God. Christ fulfilled all the hopes and aspirations of Israel. By the cross He has made the forgiveness of God, which alone brings reconciliation and peace to us, an unmistakable reality.

2. The ministry of the Spirit (1:21-22). Christ was the final and absolute affirmation of God's promises. How can men know that God is faithful? Can they know that He has kept His word? Laying bare his own heart, the apostle declared that he himself had experienced the fulfillment of God's promises. God was the basis of his Christian assurance. It was God who established him in the faith and directed his life.

God had used him mightily in the ministry and had given him the Holy

Spirit, the mark of all believers in Christ. God had directed his decisions through the Spirit. Three precious words are used to describe the ministry of the Holy Spirit.

The first word is *anoint* (*chriō*, "consecrate"). Believers are anointed. As it was customary to pour holy oil on the prophets, priests, and kings of old to anoint them for service, so the Holy Spirit has come on us. We have received the same anointing with the Spirit that Christ did for His ministry. He declared:

> The Spirit of the Lord is on me, because he has anointed me to preach good news to the poor. He has sent me to proclaim freedom for the prisoners and recovery of sight for the blind, to release the oppressed, to proclaim the year of the Lord's favor (Luke 4:18-19).

So, too, we have been empowered for Christian living and service by the Holy Spirit.

The second word is *seal* (*sphragizō*, "mark," "stamp"). Sealing here is a mark of ownership. The indwelling Holy Spirit is the common mark of all believers. His presence marks us out from the rest of mankind as those who really belong to God. Paul wrote: "The Spirit himself testifies with our spirit that we are God's children" (Rom. 8:16). We are bought at a price (1 Cor. 7:23) and the Holy Spirit bears witness to God's ownership and loving care of us.

The third word is *deposit* (*arrabon*, "downpayment," "pledge"). God has put the Holy Spirit in the hearts of His servants. That is His pledge, His downpayment, His earnest money of what we will receive on the resurrection morning. A promise can be a matter of mere words. We have not only a promise but a pledge, the Holy Spirit, "guaranteeing what is to come." Thus the Holy Spirit points back to a first-century event, the cross of reconciliation, and to a coming event, the second coming, when we will enjoy our full inheritance secured by the Savior. Life now in the Spirit is the pledge and the first installment of the life in Heaven.

C. His Reason for Postponing the Visit (1:12—2:4)

The proposed visit had been canceled because Paul feared the pain it might cause. He did not want to pay his Corinthian friends "another painful visit." His first visit occurred when the church was founded (Acts 18:6-13). Apparently he had already made a second visit, which had turned out to be an unpleasant experience.[6] But he was preparing for a third when he heard that trouble was brewing in the church.

---

[6]The second visit must have fallen between 1 Corinthians and 2 Corinthians.

There were those who were opposing him. If he had gone, he would have had to take strong disciplinary action. He put himself under an oath and called God to punish him if he lied. His desire was to offer them pastoral care, but not to lord it over their faith. If they stood at all as Christians, they would have to stand in faith; but it could not be compelled. Like any good pastor, the apostle respected his flock and wanted to clear up any misunderstanding. As a matter of fact, his purpose was not to hurt them but to help them find joy in their faith. Should he have grieved them who would have been left to make him glad? Their growth in the Lord gladdened his heart. Their joy was his joy. When he first came to Corinth, there was no Christian community; but through his ministry a church came into existence as one of God's new creations. He took delight in any success of that community.

On the "painful visit" he had been saddened. His children in Corinth were still rebellious. A visit at that time would have provoked more trouble. He did not want to come to Corinth until they had changed their attitude. This was not a matter of his own interest. On their account he wanted to enjoy a happy season with them. This would be good for them. So he wrote the "stern letter," not out of wounded pride, though his heart had been broken, but out of love which sometimes must be firm, even stern. His concern was to restore them to fellowship with him. This was the love of a pastor, flowing from Calvary, reconciling men to one another.

V. A PLEA FOR A PENITENT OFFENDER (2:5-11)

One among the Corinthians had especially caused trouble and had been excluded from the church.[7] Paul begged them to forgive and restore him to the circle of the community. The steps designed for his full restoration to fellowship were:

A. His Punishment (2:6)

The man had been reproved by the church. This action was sufficient. The church had to exercise discipline. Not only had it taken a moral stand but also

---

[7]Paul did not name the offender. The readers knew who he was. It is not likely that he was the immoral man of 1 Corinthians 5. The fact that Paul says that he had been punished enough distinguishes him from the man who had been "handed over to Satan." The offender had likely flaunted Paul's authority, about which at first the church did nothing.

had expressed it by expelling the man from the fellowship of believers. Some thought a more severe punishment should have been imposed. Paul felt it was adequate and had lasted long enough. There has to be discipline. It must never be vindictive or harsh but always tempered with love.

B. His Forgiveness and Comfort (2:7-8)

The main thing now was forgiveness. The church had been obedient to Paul in dealing with the offender. The discipline had brought him to his senses and to heartfelt contrition. The gracious task of the church was to forgive and comfort him. What the church did was to spring out of real love. Accordingly Paul urged them to reaffirm their love for the offender and to show him kindness.

Sometimes it is more difficult to forgive than to punish. Forgiveness of those who err is to be in response to God's grace. "The ethics of forgiveness keeps discipline from becoming a harsh justice of an eye-for-eye, just as the ethics of discipline keeps forgiveness from a soft—and finally cruel—indulgence."[8]

C. His Restoration (2:9-11)

The decision to reinstate the offender was left with the church, but Paul assured them, "If you forgive anyone, I also forgive him." His call for forgiveness of the offender was not simply to dispose of an awkward situation nor to pacify the man. As a matter of fact the reason Paul bade the church to restore the man was twofold: The first was "...that he will not be overwhelmed by excessive sorrow" (v. 7). The repentant could have been driven to despair if the Christians had under the pretense of doing their duty refused to restore him. Swallowed up by his remorse he could have felt cut off from God and could have abandoned his faith. Discipline has ceased to be Christian where it is so severe as to leave no place for reconciliation and a return to the warmth and security of Christian fellowship. Holiness is God's standard, but true biblical holiness is tempered by mercy and love and is sensitive to the distinction between sin and the sinner.

The second reason for restoration was the welfare of the entire church. Forgiving and reinstating the wrongdoer was not only in his interest but also for the good of the church. Paul had freely forgiven the man "for your sake." His desire was to build up the Corinthian church. The danger of an unforgiv-

---

[8]Waldo Beach, *The Christian Life*, p. 86.

ing spirit was that it could have driven the repentant wrongdoer to desperation. More than that, it would provide Satan ("adversary") with opportunity to "outwit (*pleonekteō*, "exploit," "take advantage")[9] us," that is, the church. Satan schemes to fill believers with a spirit of harshness. Of course, if the repentant sinner were overwhelmed by excessive sorrow, Satan would have an advantage over him and the church. When Christians hold grudges, Satan wins a victory. An unforgiving spirit mars the good name of the church and gives rise to divisions and bitterness. Strife and lovelessness in the church means either that the members do not practice what they preach or the gospel has no power. That gives ground to the cunning of the arch-deceiver who seeks to play havoc in the church and to turn good into evil. Moral indignation, prompted by the desire for the purity of the church can easily become self-righteousness that reveals itself in a harsh, cold, unforgiving, pharisaical spirit. To give up the effort to restore and reconcile the backslider is to abandon the way of Christ. Should that be, Satan has outwitted us and has won an advantage. That means a gain for Satan but a setback for the church.

VI. CONCLUSION

Most Christians know firsthand the hard realities of life, but at the same time the joys and peace of the Lord. Certainly this was true for Paul. He knew what it was to be hurt by ingratitude and disloyalty. He knew what it was to have his good intentions misunderstood and to be rejected for a time by a church for whom he felt great affection. His ministry was accompanied by many sufferings and conflicts for the sake of Christ. In the midst of all his adversities he was given comfort and consolation.

The experiences of the apostle Paul serve as guideposts for the Christian life. Moreover, his ministry provides timely hints for Christians when differences arise among themselves with others.

First, we must minister to the comfort of others. As Paul, we experience the sufferings of Christ. We know Christ both "in the fellowship of His suffering" and "in the power of His resurrection." God transforms suffering into comfort as the risen Christ exerts His power in our lives. Our suffering in Christ is not only transformed into comfort for us, but it also flows over and from us for the comfort of others. Suffering is part of the fabric of life. It is normal in the life of

---

[9]Also *pleonekteō* means literally "to exploit" in 2 Corinthians 7:12; 12:17-18; 1 Thessalonians 2:5.

the church. There is nothing in physical pain or sorrow which in itself insures spiritual growth and produces holiness. However, when God comforts us in our tribulations and grief, He ordains us to a ministry of comfort to others in trouble. We can carry to others the comfort received in an experience in which God gave us the victory. The ministry of comfort is open to each of us.

Second, we must not allow a credibility gap to exist. We may be charged with insincerity, accused of double-talk, and ascribed hidden motives for good work. We must remember what Jesus said:

> Therefore, if you are offering your gift at the altar and there remember that your brother has something against you, leave your gift there in front of the altar. First go and be reconciled to your brother; then come and offer your gift (Matt. 5:23-24).

Good human relations are built on mutual confidence. The foundation to such trust is to have the welfare of those whom we serve at heart and let everything be up front. Let your "yes" be "yes."

Third, we must not presume to lord over their faith. God has given us a ministry, but He has not authorized us to be tyrants, dictating beliefs, coercing conscience, and imposing obedience. Faith cannot be coerced; it is a personal matter between the individual and God. We have not been called to command but to help believers live a holy life of love, peace, and joy. We are servants of Christ, not lords over God's heritage. The practice of the ministry of reconciliation should conform to our Lord's instructions and example.

> You know that the rulers of the Gentiles lord it over them, and their high officials exercise authority over them. Not so with you. Instead, whoever wants to become great among you must be your servant, and whoever wants to be first must be your slave—just as the Son of Man did not come to be served, but to serve, and to give his life as a ransom for many (Matt. 20:25-28).

Fourth, we must exercise forgiveness. Because the church is composed of persons who are liable to sin, there is always the danger of errors in faith and living among believers. So there must be some kind of discipline to maintain holiness and love. Most parents know discipline is a part of love. A loving parent disciplines his disobedient child so that he is made aware that he is responsible for his actions. In God's family the aim of discipline is to restore the backslider to fellowship with God so that he may mature in Christ. Satan tempts us to go to either of two extremes: to be lax and tolerant of sin or to be harsh, severe, and unforgiving. Refusal to forgive the believer who has sinned and who is now repentant, or receiving him with coldness back into fellowship, works to Satan's advantage. The only way to show that he is fully restored to fellowship is to forgive, comfort, and love him. Forgiveness springs out of Christian love and strengthens the fellowship of the church as it reconciles the repentant to fellowship.

Every Christian is to be a minister of reconciliation because he has been reconciled to God and has been brought into fellowship with other believers. This fellowship is a community in which individual liberty is preserved and where members bear one another's burdens. The maintenance of harmony and peace in the fellowship of the church demands the continual process of reconciliation by which resentment and friction are overcome. United in its fellowship, the church has a vital message for a broken and disunited world.

3

The Covenant of Reconciliation

2 Corinthians 2:12—3:18

C ovenants are common enough among men. Generally they involve a mutual contract with similar commitments on either side. Marriage is described in this way. Yet a covenant may not be on equal terms, but may be a unilateral declaration. This is the kind of covenant God made with man. God initiated it and laid down the terms. His grace and love moved Him to make a covenant to redeem the Israelites (Deut. 7:6-11). The covenant stipulated that they were to be careful to keep the commandments. However, without individual commitment the covenant was not a guarantee of personal salvation. The people were to enjoy the blessings of God within the covenant community.

All the covenantal promises made to Noah, Abraham, Moses, and David expressed God's reconciling grace toward man and dealt with delivering him from sin and death. These promises, which finally focused on the line of David, were fulfilled through Jesus Christ (Luke 1:32-33). Through Him God initiated the new covenant—God was in Christ reconciling the world to Himself. This covenant accomplished what the Mosaic covenant could never do. God committed to Paul and to the church a ministry on a higher order—the ministry of the new covenant. The inspired writer, the apostle Paul, turned to the glorious nature of the new covenant ministry which for him centered in its message, the good news of reconciliation.

I. A TRIUMPHAL MINISTRY (2:12-17)

The gospel is great power. No one was more aware of this than Paul. He had seen the radical changes it made in the lives of men and its powerful moral impact on society. Yet there is no hint that he saw himself as a world conqueror or hero. His ministry was performed in deep humility and in a keen sense of dependence on God. Doors opened to him, not because of who he was but because of the gospel.

A. His Anxiety About the Church (2:12-13)

The "stern letter" had been sent to Corinth by Titus. In the meantime Paul left Ephesus and traveled north toward Macedonia, along a route where he expected to meet Titus and receive a report on conditions at Corinth. Troas was one place that the meeting might have taken place. Having arrived there, he found much encouragement. The Lord opened the door of opportunity to preach the gospel, but Titus was not there. Normally Paul would have gladly seized the opportunity with evangelistic fervor; but he could not, though the people were there, ready to be evangelized. Preoccupied with the trouble in Corinth, he had "no peace of mind" (literally, "no rest in my spirit"). So he turned his steps toward Macedonia with apparently nothing on his mind except the spiritual welfare of the Corinthians.[1]

This gives us a glimpse into the heart of the great apostle. He found no relief in his spirit from hopes and fears and prayers for his spiritual children at Corinth. He was a true pastor with a genuine love for the souls which God had committed to his care. Similar love and concern should constrain every minister of the gospel.

B. His Success Due to God (2:14)

The good news that Titus, Paul's young co-worker, brought evoked an outburst of praise: "Thanks be to God, who always leads us in triumphal procession[2] in Christ and through us spreads everywhere the fragrance of the

---

[1]Later Titus met Paul in Macedonia and gave him a good report on conditions in Corinth that relieved his anxiety. Paul does not tell of this until 7:5-7.

[2]The meaning of "leads in triumphal procession" (*thriambeuō*) is disputed. *Thriambeuō* has been variously interpreted to mean: (1) to cause to triumph; (2) to cause to triumph over someone (see Col. 2:15); (3) to lead as captives in a triumphal procession; (4) to lead as victorious soldiers in a triumphal procession. The fourth interpretation seems to be preferable in 2:14. The apostle did think of himself as a slave of Christ (Rom. 1:1) and a prisoner of Christ (Philem. 1,9), but he was

knowledge of him." In Paul's mind was the graphic picture of a Roman triumphal parade. The highest honor that could be bestowed on a victorious general in war was "a triumph." When a Roman general conquered new lands or put down a rebellion, the senate frequently gave him a magnificent triumphal procession. A holiday was declared when he and his army returned to Rome. As the general in his chariot and his army paraded, the people lined the route of the march to see the general and hail the victors. The air was filled with the fragrance of incense which was being burned and being offered to the pagan gods.

The apostle Paul viewed himself as a soldier of the victorious general, sharing in triumph. For Paul the victorious general was God, at the head of the procession. God was in Christ reconciling the world to Himself and had committed to Paul the ministry of reconciliation. So in all his missionary travel God led him and made him a sharer in the victory of Christ. The journey to Corinth became a pageant of triumph "in Christ." In every place that he reached he gave off the fragrance of the gospel of Christ. God gave him the victory. At Corinth there was a revival and conditions in the church improved. The triumphal progress of the gospel there and elsewhere was due to God's grace. Later Paul wrote: "...we are more than conquerors through him who loved us" (Rom. 8:37).

C. His Ministry Resulting in Either Life or Death (2:15-16)

The gospel is truly Christ's fragrance for all who hear it. However, Paul pointed out the double edge of the message: a fragrance of life to those being saved and a fragrance of death to those perishing.[3] During a Roman triumphal procession the aroma from the burning of incense had different effects on different people. For conquerors the fragrance meant victory and life, but for the captives, who followed in chains and were put to death at the conclusion, the fragrance was a smell of death.

The gospel can be a sweet aroma either of death unto death or life unto life.[4]

---

perfectly capable of envisioning himself as a victorious soldier "through" Christ (1 Cor. 15:57), as one who shares in Christ's victory (Rom. 8:17, 37) and as a soldier "of" Christ (Philem. 2; 2 Tim. 2:3; 4:7).

[3]The participles (*sōzomenois, apollumenois*) translated respectively "being saved," "perishing" are in the present tense and indicate that due to men's response to the gospel they are on their way either to salvation or to eternal ruin. The linear force of these participles make it clear that neither process can be thought of as complete. Both are to be consummated at the last day.

[4]The Greek literally means "a fragrance out of death unto death" and "a fragrance out of life unto life."

This depends on men's attitude toward the message of reconciliation. Those who welcome the message are put on the way that leads to the full gift of eternal life. Men who close their hearts to the gospel continue treading their way to spiritual death. Jesus himself saw men accept and reject His offer of reconciling love. Some looked on Christ and said, "My Lord and God." Others looked on Christ and said, "He hath a demon." God offers a man an undeserved gift but compels him to choose, either for life or for death. What an awesome responsibility to confront men with a message that raises eternal issues of life and death. Who is qualified for this ministry? "Who is equal to such a task?" No man in himself is qualified but God's grace is his sufficiency.

D. His Preaching from Pure Motives (2:17)

The ideal minister, the one sufficient for the ministry of Christ, is he who refuses to "water down" the Word of God. Commending his own personal example, Paul wrote: "Unlike so many, we do not peddle the word of God for profit." The word *peddle (kapēleuō)* refers to the practice of peddlers who adulterated their products and sold people cheap goods for the sake of gain. Although he was a preacher, the apostle was not selling the gospel for personal profit; but his adversaries at Corinth were merchandizing the gospel and advancing their reputations (see chapters 10-13). These people, however, claiming to be strong and equal to the ministry (2:16; 3:5), had diluted God's word in the self-interest of their hearers and for profit. In contrast Paul insisted that a minister must be sincere, without mixed motives, seeking no personal advantage; he must declare the unadulterated gospel, boldly and graciously. Only such men can be trusted with the life-and-death issues of the gospel ministry.

II. AN ACCREDITED MINISTRY (3:1-5)

Nothing is more pleasing to a faithful minister than the success of his ministry as shown in the lives of those among whom he labors. No doubt that is a genuine sign of divine commendation. God approved Paul's work. The lives of the Corinthians were a clear testimony to the success of his ministry. They had been changed by the gospel.

A. Paul's Personal Qualifications (3:1)

Letters of commendation have their place. They were as common in Paul's day as they are today. Apollos carried letters of recommendation (Acts 18:27), and

Paul had written such a letter for Phoebe to the church at Rome (Rom. 16:1). There was nothing wrong with the practice, but some wandering preachers, who cast suspicion on Paul's ministry, had reached Corinth. They had letters from churches they had visited and asked the Corinthians for testimonials to other places. These adversaries complained that Paul did not have such credentials. As might be expected, his self-defense laid him open to their vicious accusations that he was merely a braggart who delighted in praising himself. Of course he had no need of recommendations either to or from his converts. His ministry was known well by the entire church. His adversaries paraded their testimonials. So Paul, too, produced a letter.

B. His Letter of Commendation (3:2-3)

The church at Corinth was a high tribute to the ministry of Paul. God had used him to bring the Corinthians to faith and to establish the Christian community there. He made clear that this well-known church was the only commendation he needed.

1. A letter written on his heart (3:2).   Beyond dispute Paul had a letter of commendation, but this was not a document that he carried in his luggage. His letter was the Corinthian believers themselves. They were an open letter for all to see throughout the entire church, but they were inscribed on Paul's heart. Since the heart is the center of love and affection, the Corinthians were secure in his love. He was their spiritual father, and they his beloved children in Christ (1 Cor. 4:15). His relationship with them was marked by his constant affection. Everywhere he went he carried them in his heart. Likewise he should have had the same place in their heart and affections. His critics sought to win their affection and to undermine his ministry. He made it clear to them that the source of Christian life is nothing but the power of Jesus Christ.

2. A letter from Christ (3:3a).   At this point Paul shifted his attention from the Corinthians' relationship to him to their relationship to Christ. The Corinthian congregation was a letter from Christ.[5] Those people were the fruit of Paul's ministry and his influence was seen in the quality of their lives. However, no one but Christ was the author of their salvation. Christ himself had inscribed this letter, the Corinthian church.

---

[5]The genitive *(Christou)* is subjective; therefore the phrase *epistolē Christou* of verse 3 should be translated "a letter from Christ."

Letters written by us express our mind and personality. Any letter inscribed by Christ should reflect His heart and mind. The church at Corinth was Christ's letter, and Christ should be so legible in the life of each Christian as to cause men to desire the Savior. Christ was legible in the life of the dying Stephen as he prayed: "Lord, do not hold this sin against them" (Acts 7:60). Stephen's life was an open letter from Christ, seen and read by Paul and resulting in his conversion.

3. A letter written with the Spirit (3:3b).   As Christ's letter, they were "written not with ink but with the Spirit of the living God."[6] The Corinthians had had a life-changing experience in which the Holy Spirit wrote the message of Christ on them. He did not make His inscription "on tablets of stone but on the tablets of human hearts." At Mount Sinai the law was inscribed by the finger of God on tablets of stone and then given to Moses (Exod. 31:18). This external code was without power to redeem and change lives. Jeremiah foresaw the age of the new covenant when God would write the law on hearts of men by the Spirit (31:33). God had put His law in the inward parts of the Corinthians. The Word of God was written on their hearts by the Holy Spirit. As Christians they were still under solemn obligation to keep the commandments, but through the Holy Spirit they had power in themselves to keep those laws.

The Holy Spirit is the dynamic for Christian living. It is the Spirit who pours the love of God into our hearts (Rom. 5:5), prompts us to cry Abba, Father (Rom. 8:15), assists in prayer (Rom. 8:26), inspires Christian graces (Gal. 5:22), enables us to fulfill the demands of the law (Rom. 8:4), and is the "pledge" of eternal life (1:22; 5:5; Eph. 1:14). A life guided, prompted, and secured by the strong Holy Spirit is the best letter of recommendation. There is no higher recommendation of a man's ministry than the faith and dedication of those among whom he labors. For that reason the Corinthian converts bore witness to the effectiveness of Paul's ministry.

C. Divine Qualification (3:4-6)

Paul was confident that he was a fully accredited minister. Such assurance came to him "through Christ" and "of God." The life-changing experience on the road to Damascus and what Christ did for him daily made him adequate to

---

[6]The perfect participle *eggegrammenē,* "having been written" occurs in both verses 2 and 3. The force of this participle is an accomplished fact with abiding results—what had been written remains "on our hearts" and "on tablets of human hearts."

face any situation. Whatever qualification the apostle had, he knew that it was not on the basis of personal merit, since it was wholly a gift of God (1 Cor. 4:7). His judgment was that our competence is not of ourselves but that it "comes from God."

It was God who made Paul competent to be a minister of the new covenant (*diathēkē*), the new order which was instituted by Jesus Christ (Luke 22:20). What a tremendous difference the incarnation, death, resurrection, and exaltation of Jesus Christ had made in the world (1 Cor. 15:1). God's initiative to redeem the world through Christ introduces a new order in which men and women are reconciled to God, to themselves, and to one another. God had commissioned Paul to be a minister (*diakonos*, "servant," "agent") of this new order, that is, a minister not of the letter but of the Spirit. Under the old covenant the letter of the Jewish law passed the sentence of death on the sinner, but under the new covenant the Spirit gives the power and victory to all who receive the gospel.

> The difference between the old covenant and the new was that the former prescribed, the latter inspired; the former laid down the rules, the latter brought man's heart into the condition in which such rules became a part of his nature.[7]

As capable as Paul was, he was not qualified in himself. God's sufficiency made him a minister of the gospel. None of us are sufficient in ourselves to minister the new covenant. God is our sufficiency. He delights to make us capable and competent ministers of the gospel, dispensers of the new covenant ushered in by Christ.

III. A GLORIOUS MINISTRY (3:7-18)

Paul's ministry was on a higher order than the ministry of Moses. The old covenant ministered by Moses focused on the letter of the law. The Jewish law imposed rules from without and was a ministry (*diakonia*, literally meaning "service" but here referring to the order of life under the law) that brought death and condemnation. In contrast the new covenant ministered by Paul was not concerned with the letter of the law but with the Spirit and true righteousness. The teachers who sought to undo Paul's work exalted the law of Moses. They apparently taught that keeping the law was as vital to salvation as

---

[7]James C. Gray and George M. Adams, *Gray and Adams Bible Commentary*, p. 187.

faith and thus corrupted the gospel. The fact was that man could find no hope in the law. The law told him what to do, but it did not give him any strength to obey. The law cannot restore the broken relationship between God and man. The law condemns the sinner for his first offense, but the new covenant—the gospel of Christ—offers him forgiveness of all his offenses and a new reconciled life out of death.

The Corinthian believers had passed from death to life. They had been liberated from the burden of guilt. Their new life in Christ did more than testify to the success of Paul's work. It certified the superiority of the ministry of the new covenant.

A. The New Ministry Abounds in Glory (3:7-11)

The old covenant was based on the law. We can read the story of its inauguration in Exodus 34:29-35. According to the account Moses' face shone with God's glory after Moses talked with Him. The glory of God is the revelation of God, that which God makes known. Essentially His glory reveals His majesty and His power to save. The glory of God is especially connected with the deliverance of the Hebrews from Egypt (Exod. 33:17). For Isaiah the deliverance of Israel from captivity in Babylon would be a revelation of the glory of the Lord (Isa. 40:5).

God's glory was revealed in the giving of both the old covenant and the new covenant. They were both divinely established orders, but the old order was not to be compared with the new. Though the ministry of Moses was glorious, it brought condemnation and death.

How much more glorious is that which brings life and reconciles men to God and to one another. Paul enlarged upon the glory of the new order.

1. The law and gospel (3:7-8). The contrast between letter and Spirit is really between the law and the gospel. The law is lethal in its effects—"the ministry that brought death." This is exactly the purpose of the law: "...that sin might be recognized as sin..." (Rom. 7:13), "...so that every mouth may be silenced and the whole world held accountable to God" (Rom. 3:19). "The law was put in charge to lead us to Christ" (Gal. 3:24). It describes the good life which can only be realized in Christ. It also prepares us to recognize our need of Him and brings us to that condition of spiritual bankruptcy which makes Him welcome as our Savior.

The law pronounces condemnation and death, but the gospel proclaims reconciliation and life. The law says: "Cursed is everyone who does not continue to do everything written in the Book of the Law" (Gal. 3:10). The gospel says: "Blessed are they whose transgressions are forgiven, whose sins are covered. Blessed is the man whose sin the Lord will never count against him" (Rom. 4:7-8). The gospel is marked by the Spirit. The Spirit is given to everyone who receives the gospel.

2. The gospel more glorious (3:9-11).   There are two basic reasons for the gospel's surpassing the law in splendor. First, the gospel, the new covenant, bestows the free gift of righteousness.[8] The term *righteousness* is from the courtroom. God, the judge, acquits those in wrong who come before Him with faith in His Son. He is not a judge who is determined to punish the guilty. He puts them right with Himself. Thereby He creates a new order, consisting of those whose sins are forgiven and who are restored to fellowship with Him. The ministry that centers in the glorious gospel brings men into a right relationship with God and with their neighbor.

Second, the glory of the gospel is permanent. The gospel is God's last word and deed. Our Savior made it clear that it is here to stay. "Heaven and earth will pass away, but my words will never pass away" (Mark 13:31). As the glory faded from the face of Moses, so did the splendor of the old covenant. But the radiance of the gospel, the new covenant, remains. Mount Sinai was a scene of glory and revelation, but it told little about God in light of what is revealed in the gospel. The old order of Sinai faded away. However, it is still unlawful to lie, steal, or murder. The Holy Spirit works in the new order of Christian fellowship and endows believers with inner power to live the Christian life. This order will never pass away. Because of this very fact the new ministry is in every respect more glorious.

B. The New Ministry Bestowing Glory (3:12-18)

Paul had great confidence in the gospel. Such confidence was based on the abiding glory of the new covenant. Thus he had spoken boldly to his Corinthian friends. No doubt boldness of speech and action marked his ministry, but plainness of speech was not a prominent characteristic in the ministry of Moses. This was not due to any failure of his own. The truth that he mediated was largely in types and shadows and thus was often obscure. Moses had to be cautious; on the contrary, the enduring glory of the new covenant inspired

---

[8]Here "righteousness" (*dikaiosunē*) could be translated "justification." Frequently Paul employs the concept "righteousness" in stating the doctrine of justification.

Paul to bear witness with great boldness. Every Christian should be such a witness.

1. The fading glory of the old covenant (3:12-16). The old order was only temporary. This was evident when Moses received the law on the mount (Exod. 34:29-35). While he was in God's presence, his face absorbed and reflected the divine glory. When he went down to the people, they saw the radiant presence on his face. So great was the glory that they could not keep their eyes fixed on him (3:7). When Moses finished speaking, he put a veil on his face so that the Hebrews could not see the glory slowly diminish. So the glory of the old order, of the old relationship between God and man, was a fading glory. The revelation that came to Moses was true, but it was not complete. Only in the face of Jesus Christ is there full and complete revelation. The Hebrews did not understand this, for "their minds were made dull." Paul thought first of those at the foot of Mount Sinai, but then he looked down through the ages to his Jewish contemporaries who rejected the gospel. Whenever and wherever the Jews read the Old Testament, its real and true meaning was obscured because their spiritual senses were dull.

In Paul's day the Jews did not do without the veil. In the synagogue they had to place a veil on the ark of the law. For Paul that was symbolic of the fact that whenever they read the books of Moses a veil still covered their hearts. These books contain the truth, but it could not penetrate the veil over their hearts. As the Jews heard them read publicly in the synagogue, they should have been pointed to Jesus Christ; but the veil kept them from seeing that.

Their problem was not a lack of information or want of evidence. Their problem was spiritual and volitional. They refused to face the truth they had. The more men refuse God's light the harder their hearts become.

The remedy was put in simple terms: "But whenever anyone turns to the Lord (Christ), 'the veil is taken away.'" That is all that was and still is required. The turning of any man or woman to Him in faith is a sign that the veil has been removed. Everything that has stood between the believer and the Savior is set aside. There is no longer spiritual blindness. With the veil removed the Scriptures are now rightly understood, and the living Christ is seen as the fulfillment of the Mosaic law. The relation of the old order to the new covenant becomes clear.

2. The abiding glory of the new covenant (3:17-18). The preaching of the law produced condemnation. The false teaching of the Jewish intruders at Corinth did the same. The veil remained over the hearts of their hearers, but Paul's ministry produced two spiritual benefits.

a. Freedom (3:17).   For Paul, the Lord (the exalted, risen Christ) and the Spirit, though not identical, were closely related. The Spirit accompanied the preaching of the gospel and gave it power (1 Cor. 2:4; 1 Thess. 2:13), thus inscribing the truth of the new covenant on the hearts of believers (3:3).

When anyone has a personal encounter with the grace of the Lord Jesus Christ, the law of the new covenant is inscribed on his heart by the Holy Spirit. As a result, he stands free of the condemnation of the old order. For "where the Spirit of the Lord is, there is freedom."

Those who turn to the Lord experience the most blessed spiritual liberty. The iron chains of guilt which bind unbelievers are removed. When that happens there is the ability, the capacity, the freedom to serve God and our neighbor. Such freedom is not license to do as we please. Rather it is the power to do what pleases Christ. Through the Holy Spirit we are given both guidance to do what we ought and power to do what we ought. True freedom is nothing less than freedom from the bondage of fear, lust, pride, and selfishness so that we may live in the service of others. Paul summed up the purpose of Christian freedom in Galatians 5:13: "For you were called to freedom, brethren; only *do not turn* your freedom into an opportunity for the flesh, but through love serve one another" (New American Standard). The purpose of freedom is service which promises love and reconciling care of one another. The secret of freedom is the indwelling of the Holy Spirit who leads us day by day in loving obedience to God and binds us together.

b. Transformation (3:18).   All of us who turn to the Lord are made free by the Spirit and by Him we perceive the unveiled Christ of the gospel. Unlike Moses our faces are never veiled. The veil has been taken away. As Moses radiated God's glory when his face was uncovered, so we reflect Christ's glory. The word *reflect* may literally mean "to reflect as a mirror." According to Paul God has given us "the light of the knowledge of the glory of God in the face of Christ" (4:6).

The glory of God disclosed in the face of Christ is His grace and salvation. Christ's saving grace enters into us and spiritually transforms our lives so that the reflection of His glory is more than surface matter. The inner recesses of our lives are constantly being transformed into the likeness of our Savior "with ever-increasing glory."[9] The new birth and Christian growth are produced by

---

[9]The verb *being transformed (metamorphoumetha)* is in the present tense, indicating that transformation is an ongoing process. The beginning of transformation is in the new birth (John 3:3, 5). Everlasting glory *(apo doxēs eis doxan)* literally means "from glory unto glory" and is realized as the believer becomes spiritually more Christlike.

the creative power of the Holy Spirit. "For it is God who works in you to will and to act according to his good purposes" (Phil. 2:13). We, too, must work out our salvation, which is working out what God works in us. The very likeness of Christ is produced by the Holy Spirit. By the Holy Spirit the veil is removed—every barrier such as prejudice and selfishness in our hearts are put down if we are open day by day to the ministry of the Holy Spirit.

The process of transformation is not easy. It involves struggles and battles with the enemy. Self-discipline is vital to the transforming influence of the Holy Spirit in us. When we practice discipline of a dedicated life, allowing the Holy Spirit to guide us, the result is sure. The Holy Spirit gradually puts forth His fruit in our lives (Gal. 5:22-23) and more and more Christ's own likeness, His love, and forgiveness, which are best seen in the glory of the cross, are reflected in us.

IV. CONCLUSION

A truly spiritual ministry is the ministry of the new covenant. Among some today the ministry has lost its glory, but God has committed to the church the glorious ministry of the new covenant. The splendor of this ministry shines from the cross where God in Christ acted in a decisive way to mend and restore broken relationships. Nothing will surpass the radiance of the reconciling work of Christ and the mighty presence of the Holy Spirit in the hearts of believers. The covenant ministered by Moses gave great prominence to the letter of the law, but its glory was temporary and limited.[10] The glory of the new covenant is everlasting. There is glory for those who live close to God and minister in the demonstration and power of the Holy Spirit.

Paul reflected on this ministry into which God sent him. He dealt with matters that are really important to the ministry today.

First, the recognition that our competence for ministry comes from God. Our confidence should not lie in our own competence, but in what God does to make us competent. Regardless of how excellent our talents and skills are, no one can bear alone the weight of the Christian ministry. The task is so great, but our personal resources are too small. We grow weary and fainthearted, because the task seems impossible at times. There is often more to do in the church than our time and energies will allow. But thank God the whole enterprise of the ministry does not rest on our shoulders.

---

[10]This is no reflection on the Old Testament. It, too, is the Word of God.

It does not please God for us to labor under the "messiah complex," thinking that the salvation of the world depends on us. At times we do well to pause, to relax, and to pray for understanding that our work is truly the Lord's work. We have the enduring assurance: "...our competence comes from God. He has made us competent as ministers of a new covenant..." (3:5-6). We are not creators of our skills in ministry, regardless of how highly trained we may be. Our qualifications and skills for ministry are all God-given. Our natural gifts are gifts from Him, and the full use of them is possible only as they are enriched and employed by the Holy Spirit (1 Cor. 12-14). Whatever our gifts, let us be aware that they are not of merit but of grace. There is no basis for pride in our accomplishments. Our only boast is in the Lord. God is our sufficiency. God alone can call, train, and use us as His servants. As He does, we become capable, efficient ministers of the new covenant.

Second, the highest ministerial recommendation is the lives that have been changed through our ministry. Paul's preaching had served the interest of reconciliation. He was "the repairer of the breach" between God and man. Many lives at Corinth had been remarkably transformed. Those people were his credentials. They were touched by his ministry, and they were shaped and fashioned by the gospel. The very existence of the Corinthian church was all the recommendation that he needed. Its members were his letters of recommendation "known and read by everybody."

Such letters are not written with pen and ink but "with the Spirit of the living God." They are not written on paper or on tablets of stone but "on the tablets of human hearts." They are the kind of letters that are lasting tributes to our ministry. They indicate that we are truly successful servants of Christ and instruments of the Spirit. Today success in the ministry so often is not seen in biblical terms of service but in terms of the marketplace: statistics, growth, efficiency, and dollars. Our letters of recommendation are big Sunday schools, tithe records, impressive ministerial reports, bigger buildings, personal popularity, and ecclesiastical empires. None of these are our true credentials. The best ones are the people we have led out of darkness into light. Their lives bear the marks of the Holy Spirit. These are plain for all men to read. All can see that they are reconciled to life, to one another, and to God.

Third, rules and regulations have no power to deliver us from the bondage of sin. The letter of the law kills and condemns, and awakens a sense of sin and the desire of deliverance from guilt. The Mosaic law was what the deceivers preached at Corinth. For them slavish obedience to the code of law as well as faith in Christ was the ground of salvation. Mechanical observance to the outward form of the law avails nothing. Legalism still is a pitfall to vital faith in

Christ, and as always it disrupts the Christian fellowship, alienating believer from believer.

What is so vital to fellowship with God and victorious Christian living is the Holy Spirit. The Spirit makes us alive, reveals Christ to us, sets us free, pours God's love into our hearts, and baptizes us with His power. The abiding and renewing presence of the Holy Spirit transforms us into the likeness of Christ. This is a lifelong, glorious experience—"being transformed into his likeness with ever increasing glory." There is not and never has been a shortcut to holiness. Self-discipline is required as the indwelling Spirit conforms us to the likeness of Jesus. Spiritual struggles, temptations, burdens, sufferings, troubles, and doubts have been experienced by most of us as we have been fashioned in the likeness of the Lord. Transformation is never easy or smooth; but as the Holy Spirit changes us, more and more, the glory and beauty of the Lord are reflected in us. Such will be seen in:

> Reconciling differences
> Willingness to suffer for Christ
> Genuine humility
> Restoring a believer "overtaken in a fault"
> Living in fellowship "one with another"
> Striving to keep the unity of the Spirit
> Holding firmly to the truth
> Being loving in our interpersonal relationships with other believers
> Serving one another
> Preferring one another

All Christians are to be involved in such activities. All Christians are to be ministers of reconciliation—ministers of the new covenant. The covenant of reconciliation was initiated by God through His Son, Jesus Christ, and is expressed in the Spirit. God has "made his light to shine in our hearts to give us the light of the knowledge of the glory of God in the face of Christ" (4:6). The Spirit brings freedom and transforms us into the likeness of Christ with ever-increasing glory (3:17, 18).

4

The Ministry and Men of Clay

2 Corinthians 4:1-18

What is a minister of the gospel? A talented person? A man with a super personality? A man with all the answers? An eloquent speaker? A gifted administrator? Most ministers are none of these, but they are men of fallibilities, weaknesses, frailties, and troubles common to other mortal men. The most devoted men and women of God are not insulated from human limitations and frustrating conflict. These are the cause of a high percentage of ministerial dropouts. Many of God's servants have left the ministry because of contentious believers who create strife over petty concerns. Their idealism has been worn thin by encounters with selfish, stubborn, and immature Christians.

The great apostle Paul was exposed to these in his ministry. Most of us see his work in terms of power and strength, and rightly so. But as gifted as he was, he himself knew what it was to be weak and insufficient to bear the burdens and troubles of his calling. He did not, however, become a ministerial dropout. By God's mercy he had been saved and called to the ministry of reconciliation. He was "a frail vessel of the earth," but the power of God triumphed through his weaknesses. He learned that when he was not so successful God had a better chance to shine forth. The great power of God does not rest on the power of man—not on his impressive appearance, popularity, persuasiveness, or intellectual accomplishments. These characteristics devoted to God are of use;

but our weaknesses, as well as strengths, are used by God to bring new reconciled life and to build fellowship among believers.

I. THE MINISTRY OF PROCLAIMING THE GOSPEL (4:1-6)

Every person who ministers at some time is tempted to lose heart. Problems may seem to be overwhelming and personal weariness may appear too great to bear. There may be stubborn indifference, even hard core antagonism in the church where we serve. Critics within the church tie our hands so that little is accomplished. What Paul encountered at Corinth was not different. He was not overwhelmed. He was disturbed, but he did not despair. He knew that the call of God was on his life. God had saved him and had given him a ministry that could change a lot of things—the person, the church, and the world. He took courage in living and declaring the powerful gospel that heals divisions and restores broken relationships.

A. Honesty and Sincerity in Life and Message (4:2a)

The integrity of Paul's ministry had been challenged.[1] In response to the charges, he set forth the characteristics of a true minister. First, he gave no place to underhanded ways. There was nothing for him to conceal. He had "renounced secret and shameful ways." He had no use for deception in his methods and dealings with people. People look for ministers to be free of cunning duplicity, to be devoted servants of Christ, to work effectively at the cure and care of souls, and to help them to deal with alienation, loneliness, hurts, failure, and suffering. To their disappointment and hurt they may find instead an "operator." The ministerial operator does not have a shepherd's heart. His ministry is not motivated by the desire to restore the lost and bind up the wounds of the broken hearted. He is a gifted politician in church affairs, well schooled in the art of manipulation. He knows how to work the system for his own advantage. Under the guise of being religious, he strives to further his selfish ends. His success pains those who love and serve the Church.

Second, Paul did not tamper with the Word of God. A minister needs all the light he can get on the Scriptures, but he should handle the Word of God with

---

[1]This is implied by what Paul said rather than being explicitly stated in 4:2f.

great care. Fanciful interpretations should be given no place. Such cater to the sensational and are designed to draw the crowds and supposedly explain what God has left as mystery. The temptation to use Scripture as a convenient springboard to get on a hobbyhorse is always real. This blunts the edge of the message and adulterates the gospel.

That is precisely what Paul's rivals did. They distorted the gospel and went beyond what the gospel required—faith in Christ for salvation. They made obedience to the law as important as faith in Christ. The issue was Christian liberty, the crux of the Reformation church struggle. Martin Luther was a great champion of freedom in Christ—freedom from the yoke of the law. His text was: "The righteous will live by faith" (Rom. 1:17), which ruled out human deeds of any kind as a basis for acceptance with God. The demands of the gospel must be adhered to, but we must be careful not to go beyond the Word of God. The minister who erects standards for Christian living that are of his own construction distorts the gospel. He goes beyond what Scripture requires and is prone to be harsh and severe. Such an approach creates strife and disagreement that divide and wound the body of Christ. The gospel needs to be declared frankly and clearly, but there needs to be balance in our preaching and witnessing.

B. A Positive Affirmation (4:2b)

The gospel is a message for all men—not just for people with special intellectual gifts and spiritual insight. The apostle was devoted to proclaiming plainly the unadulterated truth.[2] He knew that the truth of the gospel could put the fragmented life of any man or woman back together. Care was taken not to appeal to the prejudices of men, but he declared the truth in good faith. There was no question of his seeking the approval of a small group or of catering to the whims of the few. His message was for the sincere conscience of the ordinary man.

To every kind of human conscience, whether instructed or uninstructed, clear or dull, friend or foe, he commended the sincerity and truth of his preaching. His life and motives lay open. He had nothing to hide. Christ had granted him authority for ministry. He had not misused it. He had not forced it on others. Every man and woman of God should renounce entirely any use

---

[2]The fact that Paul in verse 2 used *truth* (*aletheia*) rather than *gospel* (*euangelion*) is significant. *Truth* has a broader meaning than *gospel*. He commended himself not by creating tales about himself but by stating plainly the truth. Compare 12:6.

of power that betrays their ministry of love and service. Imposing our will on others provokes conflict and alienation. Paul did not fall into that temptation. He chose to commend his authority, that is, to make it known to help others to accept what he was saying in Christ's name and to make his appeal to every man's conscience.

C. The Blindness of Unbelievers to the Gospel (4:3-4)

Paul was a true and faithful messenger. Should not all men have believed his message? Some who heard him preach, however, did not come to faith in Christ. Why? Was he at fault? Did he fail to make the gospel clear? Or was the gospel itself at fault? Could the gospel really enable men to call off their hostilities toward God and one another and be at peace with themselves?

It was not Paul's fault or the gospel's. Men were and still are responsible to God for rejecting the gospel. Paul did not excuse unbelief. Earlier he spoke of a veil on the hearts of Jews who rejected the gospel (3:15). Here the gospel is veiled to those on their way to destruction. The gospel was unveiled in Paul's preaching. So it was their hearts that were veiled, not the gospel itself. Their response to the message had shut out the gospel light. Hughes reminds us:

> The fault, however, is not in the gospel, but in those who have failed to discern its glory. The unveiled gospel, openly proclaimed, has been veiled to them because it is veiled in them: the veil is over their hearts and minds (3:14ff.), not over the gospel. It is not Paul's gospel but they who stand condemned. The absence of its saving effects in their lives shows that they are perishing in blind unbelief, while its glory continues undiminished.[3]

There was another power at work blinding men to the gospel. Those persisting in unbelief had become a victim of Satan, "the god of this age." Christ by His victory over sin and death has broken the grip of Satan (Col. 1:13; 2:15). He is a defeated foe, but Satan remains a powerful adversary of God in this present world order. The results of Christ's victory are not yet complete. Only believers now know something of it. By Christ they have been rescued from the "present evil age" (Gal. 1:4). Satan blinds the minds of unbelievers and hinders them from seeing the light of the gospel. These people are not honest doubters or seekers after the truth. They bow down before the prince of dark-

---

[3]Philip E. Hughes, *The Second Epistle to the Corinthians*, (The New International Commentary on the New Testament), p. 125.

ness and choose a godless way of life. They do not come to faith because they do not want to believe in Christ. They deliberately choose to continue their vendetta against God. Their way of life alienates them from true moral and spiritual values. Their gods may be money, power, popularity, success, and prestige. These things do not permanently satisfy. They can do nothing about man's desperate spiritual needs. He is estranged from God, estranged from himself, and estranged from his neighbor. There is no hope for him but in Jesus Christ.

The dreadful result of willful and persistent rebellion is that Satan blinds rebels to the truth of the gospel. This is their own fault. Sin leads to blindness: "...they cannot see the light of the gospel of the glory of Christ...." Being in darkness, they do not see the light streaming from the gospel. The gospel throws light on God; it discloses Him as a Father. In the life and death of Christ this light shines the brightest. Christ is the light and glory of God. In Him God became visible (John 1:18). In Him we see the very image of God (John 14:9). He reveals the nature and character of God. At the same time He is in the image of man also. He is the God-man. In Him God and man meet and are reconciled. The gospel proclaims that Christ is the living source of love, of reconciliation, of peace. Unbelievers, persisting in rebellion against God, are blind to who Christ is, as was Paul before his conversion.

D. The Mission of the Minister (4:5-6)

The servant of the Lord is not an ecclesiastical lord. There is no place in a genuine evangelical ministry for self-exaltation, self-glorification. The world says, "Exalt yourself," but according to the Savior the way to true greatness is to "humble yourself"—"crucify yourself." Paul stated two significant truths relevant to this.

First, the minister is to herald Christ, the crucified and risen Lord. The Savior cannot be center stage when the minister magnifies himself and proclaims his own thoughts and doctrine. Pomp has no place in the work of the Lord. Ministers are to declare Jesus as Lord of the church and themselves as servants of others. They have not been called to be lords over anyone. There is but one Lord—Jesus Christ. Ministers are "servants because of Jesus' sake."

Ministers are to seek service, not sovereignty. The truth is that human nature relishes control over people. The love of power is not far behind the love of money. This touches the church and its leaders. The temptation for ministers to become lords is great. When a man of God yields, he assumes a dictatorial one-man rule. Every minister needs to be a real leader—a man who has vision, sets goals, sees them through to completion, even when stepping on a few toes in the process. However, leadership and bossism must not be confused. A leader who shares his authority with others can be outvoted, but a boss insists on his way regardless of the opposition's strength. The self-styled boss is nothing but an autocrat, determined to make himself sovereign.

When we are tempted to become bosses, to have our way in the church, we need to turn to the cross to behold the Servant of servants whose whole life was one of ministry. He gave Himself unselfishly to those who needed Him. Our "attitude should be the same as that of Jesus Christ: Who ... made himself nothing, taking the very nature of a servant" (Phil. 2:5, 7).

Second, God redeems men through Christ. This was Paul's experience. As he trod the path to Damascus, God flooded his heart with the brilliant light of reconciling grace. It was as real as the light when God at creation said: "Let there be light" (Gen. 1:3). The same God caused the light of the gospel to shine in Paul's heart. It was then that the man of Tarsus met the man of Nazareth. He was a proud Pharisee; but he was not a godless man, not given to his own passions and lusts. He seemed to be in every way a creditable man—"circumcised on the eighth day, of the people of Israel, of the tribe of Benjamin, Hebrews of Hebrews," a pupil of Gamaliel thoroughly trained in the law of the fathers and zealous for God[4]—but he was in darkness. Spiritual light dawned in his heart and dispelled the darkness of ignorance. He became a new man, radically changed by Christ. So he declared: God "made his light shine into our hearts to give us the light of the knowledge of the glory of God in the face of Christ." What happened to him was of God. A little later in the epistle he wrote: "All this is from God, who reconciled us to himself through Christ and gave us the ministry of reconciliation" (5:18).

This was the ministry Paul and the church received. At the center of it is a person—the Lord Jesus Christ. The nature of our ministry is "the glory of God in the face of Jesus Christ." God has caused light to shine in our hearts so that we might see and then proclaim the knowledge of God's glory. This ministry is not something to be enjoyed selfishly, not something to be used to exalt self. There is a "cheap" ministry in which one serves without being spent. Service becomes self-glorification, self-proclamation, pomp, and show. In the Bible service is always costly. Its heart is suffering, self-giving, and personal sacrifice. The temptation to be satisfied simply with the enjoyment of God's blessings is ever present. But our responsibility is to share with others what we have seen

---

[4]See Philippians 3:5 and Acts 22:3.

in the glorious face of Jesus Christ—His meekness, kindness, longsuffering, forgiveness, love; His authority over the powers of sin and Satan; the mystery of reconciliation through His death and resurrection; and His acceptance into fellowship the alienated, the restless, the brokenhearted, the wounded, and the scarred.

II. THE MINISTRY TESTED BY SUFFERINGS (4:7-18)

Christ had led Paul into the Christian life and called him to an unselfish ministry. The credit for this did not belong to the apostle. It was not due to his powers as a preacher. He and his co-workers were but frail and unworthy vessels whom God used.

A. Treasure in Vessels of Clay (4:7)

There were vessels made of gold and silver but the least among the vessels were those made of clay or earthenware. Paul had received treasure, the precious gospel; but he was still no more than a vessel of clay, a mortal man. It was a great privilege for him to be a Christian minister. However, he was still involved in the human situation. He was still subject to the chances and changes of life. He still had a weak, fragile, mortal body. His rivals mocked him for his weak appearance and ineffective speech (10:1, 10). They dismissed his view of the ministry as ridiculous (chapters 10-13). He told them how adversity must be received when the minister desires to serve: ". . . for Christ's sake, I delight in weaknesses, in insults, in hardships, in persecutions, in difficulties. For when I am weak, then I am strong" (12:10). He endured alienation and suffering while living through conflict and clash of positions (2:1-3; 7:8-10).

At times of stress he must have had real spiritual problems. His emotions must have been spent. His hope and enthusiasm must have been emptied. During times of alienation and loneliness his ministry must have appeared to be barren and void. No doubt Paul was of tough fiber. No man could have gone through all that Paul suffered with unbroken health. He was harassed by a recurrent ailment—"a thorn in my flesh" (12:7). He was shipwrecked, stoned, beaten with rods, etc. (11:24-27). So he knew the frailty of the body and the pain of suffering.

Like all ministers Paul was a vessel of clay. That was no barrier to God's purpose, however. Rubies and diamonds of the earth would have been placed in the finest vessels. God entrusted His most precious treasure, the gospel, to weak, clay vessels like Paul. There was a reason: "...to show that this all-surpassing power is from God and not from us." Here is a theology of Christian weakness, which we would all do well to ponder. God breaks through our human weakness. Through weakness God triumphs. Our weaknesses bring to light the power of Christ as the real force that makes us successful ministers. Weakness should not be seen as a hurdle that must somehow be overcome before we can serve effectively. Personal weakness and troubles in ministry are frequently God's opportunity. It is not uncommon for Him to shine through when our physical powers are drained, when our emotions are emptied, when our perspective is confused. "Power beyond" produces the results and enables us to be genuine ministers of reconciliation.

The exceeding greatness of Christ's power overcomes weakness. It goes beyond and far exceeds it. It converts weakness to strength. "We are more than conquerors through him who loved us" (Rom. 8:37). It is our frailty that leads us to the power of Christ which triumphs over weakness. It is our weakness that opens us to the experience of all-sufficiency of God's grace. I have seen men and women with great handicaps do outstanding work in the kingdom of God. Some were blind, some crippled; others had speech impediments; still others had limited backgrounds in education. Through their weakness and inabilities the Spirit worked. The power of Christ overcame their weakness and made them effective workers of God. They were good stewards of the treasure entrusted to them in pots of clay. All that God needs are dedicated men and women who will allow His power to work through them.

B. Encouragement in Deep Distress (4:8-10)

The apostle was exposed to a succession of desperate crises in his ministry. Though a weak vessel he was never brought to defeat. There was always strength from God. He described four such situations.

1. He was hard pressed on every side but not crushed.   The situation was that of hostile forces pressing in on him. He found himself in desperate straits. There seemed to be no way out. He was locked in and hard pressed from every side. God provided a way out. A particular example is when Paul came to Macedonia (7:5-7). He was in a terrible dilemma—pressed on every side and had no rest. The good news Titus brought from Corinth gave him comfort and joy. It gave him a way out of the perplexing circumstances. There are no dead ends in the service of God. He opens up a way.

2. He was perplexed but not in despair.   Mounting church problems and growing opposition perplexed Paul. At times, he had no idea of what to do nor where to go. He was bewildered and confused. He was at the end of his own resources, but God's resources had not been exhausted; therefore he never gave way to ultimate despair. He never lost hope or surrendered in the fight. No Christian should be reduced to utter despair. There is God's grace; therefore there is hope.

3. He was persecuted but not abandoned.   The agony of being hated and persecuted by enemies was not uncommon to Paul. At Corinth he had to face fierce adversaries of the gospel. At times his enemies overtook him and struck him down. He did not exaggerate when he spoke of being "exposed to death again and again" (11:23). Indeed a remarkable instance occurred when Jewish adversaries from Antioch and Iconium pursued him to Lystra. There they stoned him. After dragging his body out of the city, they left him for dead. Regardless of the form his suffering took—physical hardships, loneliness, alienation issuing from church trouble—he was conscious of the presence of God. It might have appeared to human eyes that he was abandoned. Yet he himself never felt that he was. When he was placed on trial for his life, everyone deserted him. "But," he wrote, "the Lord stood at my side and gave me strength" (2 Tim. 4:17). God's servants may be forsaken by their friends as well as persecuted by enemies, but He Himself will never forsake them.

4. He was struck down but not destroyed.   This implies more than a physical assault. The Corinthian church caused him personal pain. The rebellion and strife of his converts were a devastating blow at his heart. He was knocked down, but he was never knocked out.[5] Great sorrow and anxiety are disabling even to God's servants, but these trials do not prove to be fatal. God stands by and delivers His servants from what would be too severe.

These are some of the great paradoxes of the Christian life. Part of the secret to Paul's success as a servant of Christ was his attitude toward suffering. "The ministry of reconciliation begins with a positive attitude concerning the situation in which we find ourselves. Though we cannot ignore the disagreeable aspects, we believe that God can turn even these to serve His gracious purpose."[6] Pain and suffering which belong to life remind us of human frailty; but there is God, in His all-surpassing power, through whom we triumph.

[5]See the New Testament in Modern English (Phillips).
[6]Morris A. Inch, *My Servant Job*, p. 116.

C. The Pattern of Death and Life (4:10)

Paul's life, as well as his preaching, was a clear witness to the gospel. His own lifestyle reflected the death and resurrection of the Savior. All ministers should carry out Christ's ministry of humble service and suffering. What did this involve for Paul?

First, he was always carrying in his body the death of Jesus. *Always* emphasizes the process. "I have been crucified with Christ," he wrote the Galatians;[7] but he spoke of "becoming like him in his death"[8]—a process not yet complete. He knew that he died once to sin, but that he always carried around in his body the dying of the Lord. His sufferings and hardships were a lingering kind of death. Day by day his ministry made death more and more a reality. Experiences common to the ministry can also make us conscious of the same process of dying. As we endure adversity and crises for Jesus' sake, we share with him in His death.

Second, he shared with Christ's death so that the life of Jesus could also be revealed in his body. The continual risking of his life was that others might be led to the Savior. Through his ministry "the life of Jesus" was manifested to those who believed his message. Paul had communion with both "the death of Jesus" and "the life of Jesus." As a frail vessel he carried about the dying of Jesus—the perils common to his ministry. At the same time he experienced constant deliverance and renewal of his courage. Those were manifestations of resurrection life. All believers will ultimately and finally be resurrected, but the glorious life of the risen Christ is manifested already in their lives. The bodies of believers have not been redeemed yet, but now in this world are signs of resurrection life. The Holy Spirit brings freedom (3:17) and sets believers free from the old self. They "are being renewed day by day" (4:16).

Suffering discipleship—the carrying "around in our body the death of Christ"—provides occasion for the manifestation of new life in our present frail existence. At any time vessels of clay can be broken. Paul was keenly aware of this possibility. This did not deter him in his ministry. He laid his life on the line for no other reason than to touch hearts of others with "the life of Jesus." His purpose for experiencing the dying Jesus in his body was to reveal the life of Jesus to others. His life was poured out in service to build up the Church. Every Christian, in fact the whole Church, needs to be drawn into

---

[7]Galatians 2:20.
[8]Philippians 3:10.

the same ministry. Our task is to manifest to others "the life of Jesus." If we preach the gospel for any other reason our motives are not right. We are building monuments to ourselves. Our goal becomes success, defined more in terms of church statistics, large budgets, and brick-and-mortar concerns than in manifesting the life of Jesus and involvement in the task of reconciliation. The crying need is for all to die out to selfish ambitions. For the reconciling of the world God has done enough in Christ. However, we are called to take up the cross. A sacrificial life, as well as the declarations of the Word of God, manifests the life of Jesus so that others may share in the abundant life the Savior came to bring.

D. The Secret Source of Endurance and Victory (4:11-18)

Paul was a frail vessel, but the power of God enabled him to live through great difficulties. He did not wish the Corinthians to think that the gospel was powerful because he was impressive. He was weak and only a winner because of God.

1. A sacrificial life (4:11, 12, 15). There were those at Corinth who were tempted to despise the frailty of Paul. Their rich experiences in Christ had come to them through his sufferings. As a minister he not only preached about the sufferings of Jesus, but he had personally experienced them—"always being given over to death." His ministry put him in situations full of danger. He lived what he preached—the death and resurrection of Christ. Not that he enjoyed dying and rising again, especially since they demanded inner death week after week. But he practiced what he invited others to practice. For him sorrow, anxieties and persecutions were not due to fate or misfortune. He accepted them and lived a sacrificial life for two reasons.

The first was "for Jesus' sake." His consuming desire was to serve Jesus. Until he departed for heaven his ambition was to be found in the service of the One who suffered and died and yet rose and now reigns as Lord. He was ready to make the necessary sacrifices. There is no other way to have a fruitful ministry. Ministerial success demands that we be spent in the care of people and in meeting their deep spiritual needs. Men and women who know the difficulties and count the cost make better ministers.

The second was for the sake of the Corinthians. "All this," he said, "is for your benefit." What he endured was for the advantage of his people. He followed in the footsteps of the Good Shepherd who laid down his life for his sheep (John 10:11). As a good minister, Paul gladly spent himself in service, not for his own sake, but for the sake of the church. His aim was twofold: (1) The building up of the church—that God's reconciling grace would reach more and more people. Only His grace can meet the need of people who have not learned to forgive, people whose lives are full of bitterness and hatred, people who are frustrated, fragmented, and alienated from God and man. (2) The glory of God. He desired that all of his successes redound to the glory of God. When God's reconciling grace and love become real to the hearts of people, the response necessarily is to thank Him and thus to praise and glorify Him.

2. A strong faith and hope (4:13, 14). Faith does not keep silent. What Paul believed he spoke. What he sincerely believed was the gospel, and he sincerely preached it. It is not enough to speak. Words can be empty, nothing but meaningless phrases. Preaching and teaching need to be permeated with utter sincerity and conviction of heart. The sincerity of Paul was inspired by a strong hope: "We know that the one who raised the Lord Jesus from the dead will also raise us with Jesus and present us with you in his presence." He knew that beyond earthly afflictions and tribulations lies God's victory. The solid ground for his confidence was the resurrection of Jesus. It guarantees the resurrection of his people. Every trace of separation will be removed and every believer will be brought into perfect fellowship with his Lord. We who belong to Him will continue to belong to Him, even on the other side of death. We will, therefore, be raised with Jesus, so as to be with Him forever (1 Thess. 4:17).

Why did Paul not lose courage and faith? He was only a frail man. He faced tremendous difficulties. He worked under great strain. Through it all he remained a faithful servant and full of hope. The reason was hidden from the gaze of man—the inner man was constantly renewed. Outwardly he grew old. His physical strength was gradually running out because of the wearing stresses, strains, and hardships of the ministry. But day by day there was the renewal of spiritual strength. The inner man was strengthened by the Holy Spirit, by the promises of the Word of God, and by prayer and communion with Christ. The body wears down—the eyes grow dim, limbs lose their strength, and the memory becomes faulty, but the inner man can be strengthened and renewed daily. The secret is a day-by-day fellowship with the Lord. Knowing Him involves a relationship. It is more than membership in a church or church attendance. It is a matter of relationship from day to day. Jesus calls us to deny self and follow Him daily. Christianity is a day-by-day religion. A daily walk with the living Lord makes us know what He can do. We are spiritually strengthened by constant fellowship with Him.

3. A spiritual vision (4:17-18).   Eyes of faith are fixed, not on seen but on unseen things. The view of unseen things gave Paul two things. First, it gave him a true perspective. His faith in God shaped his outlook on his troubles. They were light and momentary, that is, they were nothing more than insignificant trifles. As he elsewhere said: "I consider that our present sufferings are not worth comparing with the glory that will be revealed in us" (Rom. 8:18). Not even Paul was able to describe fully the glorious inheritance that awaits believers: "No eye has seen, no ear has heard, no mind has conceived what God has prepared for those who love him" (1 Cor. 2:9). Indeed, suffering is momentary and "light in weight" in contrast to the abiding superabundant weight of the future glory.

Second, the view of unseen things gave Paul power to endure the trials of life. The only way to look at life is against God's purpose in Christ. It is there that we learn that "what is seen is temporary, but what is unseen is eternal." The present world is filled with distrust, hatred, animosity, alienation, and despair. These even show their ugly heads in the church. If we saw nothing else, we could lose heart. "But we see Jesus, who was made a little lower than the angels, now crowned with glory and honor" (Heb. 2:9).

Stephen, looking about him, saw an angry mob accusing him of blasphemy and casting stones on his prostrate body. Had he seen nothing else his heart might well have failed him. But that was not all that he saw. He "looked up to heaven and saw the glory of God, and Jesus standing at the right hand of God" (Acts 7:55). The stones crushed his body. He, too, along with Paul and many others, shared in "the sufferings of Christ" and his response was "Lord, do not hold this sin against them" (Acts 7:60). Stephen's gaze was fixed on unseen things. We need to see the same—God's reconciling love, His triumph over powers and principalities in Christ, the fruit of the Spirit—love, joy, peace, longsuffering, gentleness, goodness, faith, meekness, and temperance. These are eternal. They will never pass away.

III. CONCLUSION

The precious treasure of the gospel has been put in vessels of clay. God could have sent angels to preach the message of reconciliation, or He could have sent the noblest sons of men to teach the good news of salvation. But God chose weaker vessels so that His power might be more glorified in His upholding them and in His working through them.

God calls frail mortal men to share with others the precious gospel of Christ. Though weak we should not be bungling amateurs, but men and women fully equipped for our task, indeed in both knowledge and skill. The Word of God needs to be declared skillfully in its power and purity. As ministers we must renounce anything that might betray our ministry. We must give no place to deceptive and shameful ways. We must not distort the Word of God or handle it deceitfully. The healing of human alienations requires that our ministry be rooted in Scripture. By proclaiming the Word of God the Lord strove to overcome divisions, ruptures, and barriers that separate man from God and men from men. If we fail to proclaim and teach the Word of God, we undermine our vital role as ministers of reconciliation. We become inarticulate voices with no real message in a world seeking meaning and hope. Signs that tell us that many people desperately need to be reconciled are abundantly clear: riots and delinquency, mounting suicides, absorption in sex, increasing alcoholism and drug addiction, and rampant distrust and hostility.

These are all evidences of people's need to hear the gospel—"God was reconciling the world to himself in Christ." This is the message that pronounces judgment of sin and proclaims hope for the sinner and produces healing and wholeness. The proclamation of the same message is the true source of revival and renewal in the church. The message is powerful, but the messengers are weak. "We have this treasure in jars of clay." The cost of this ministry which God has entrusted to us cannot be evaded. Men and women of God, daily carrying their cross, meet troubles in ministry. Wherever true reconciliation takes place there is agony. It cost Christ the cross. Because of it Paul shared in the sufferings of Christ. He endured them not because they were trivial or because he was a calloused soul. Few men have ever been more sensitive to pain than he. He had no fondness for being shipwrecked or for being thrown into prison. He took no delight in being cold, hungry, and rejected.

Today ministers are confronted with a great variety of frustrating experiences: overtaxing demands of work, poor preparation for the tasks of ministry, lack of job satisfaction, loneliness, discouragement, anger, failures in counseling, frustrations due to lack of commitment and maturity of others. Failure to live out good intentions and lack of prayer add to daily disappointments. Human weakness is something with which all ministers have to reckon. The recognition of our weaknesses brings to light the fact that the power of Christ is what makes us effective and successful ministers. We serve in the power of Christ. He meets us where we are and helps us to live through pain, depression, alienation, loneliness, and anxieties—through the times when the ministry appears barren and void.

Through all these perplexities let us never lose sight of the close link between the ministry and the Holy Spirit in our lives. "Now it is God who makes both us and you stand firm in Christ. He anointed us, set his seal of ownership on us, and put his Spirit in our hearts as a deposit, guaranteeing what is to come" (2 Cor. 1:21-22). The Spirit is the guarantee for future deliverance and is present power for an effective ministry of reconciliation.

5

The Motivation for Ministry

2 Corinthians 5:1-21

A competent and successful ministry rendered for Jesus' sake is not a blind devotion to duty. It is not merely activities such as preaching, prayer, administration, and visitation. Instead the ministry is a way of life that reflects a proper view of the future as well as the present. It is a surrender of all our skills and talents to God. It is the use of what we have by the Holy Spirit to accomplish the task of evangelism and practical service. It is a work to which every Christian and the whole Church should be dedicated.

Throughout all of the troubles which came to Paul, three great doctrinal concepts spurred him to great spiritual achievements. (1) He was persuaded that a different life awaited him, a life without suffering, without change, without death. He had an abounding hope of resurrection and of heaven (5:1-8). (2) Paul was convinced of divine judgment (5:9-10). In the face of the coming judgment he had remarkable confidence, for his relation to God was already right. (3) He was persuaded that the whole work of reconciliation originated in God's love and was manifested in and effected by Jesus Christ (5:11-21). These doctrines—the resurrection, the judgment, and reconciliation—gave Paul a new incentive and inspiration for living and declaring the "message of reconciliation."

I. THE NEW BODY (5:1-8)

The apostle had looked at his adversities from a true perspective. He faced the fact of death. Death is a mystery, but for Paul it was not a step into the dark.

A. His Assurance of "A Building from God" (5:1)

"We know" indicates Paul's confidence that the Christian will eventually be done with the frailty and suffering of his present existence. The body is like a tent—frail and insecure. The tent-body which ages and gradually wears out will be taken down and folded up in death. At the moment of death when the earthly tent is destroyed we will receive a new home—"a building from God." Our old dwelling will give way to our new dwelling. This is not the final state of resurrection, but it will be one of peace and bliss (Phil. 1:21-23). Paul described this state in terms of "an eternal house in heaven" and "our heavenly dwelling." During the interval between death and resurrection we will not be homeless. We will have "a building from God"[1] and will be "at home with the Lord."

Between the time the body is buried and the resurrection the Christian is present with Christ. This intermediate state will be a temporary state. The final state will not come to realization until the second coming and the resurrection of the faithful. Then we will receive our new bodies, spiritual bodies, and our salvation will be complete. What Jesus initiated through His death and resurrection will lead finally to perfect reconciliation, to perfect salvation, and to the fulfillment of the believer's destiny.

B. His Desire for the New Body (5:2-5)

Death did not have any special attraction for Paul. He desired that Christ come before the hour of death, and he would be transformed without having to die. Consider what Paul said in regard to this hope.

First, he wanted to be clothed (5:2). He was still in the tent-body, groaning inwardly and longing constantly to be clothed with a spiritual body. His hope was not for death. That would have been unnatural. Death is not the hope of

---

[1]It is difficult to explain exactly the difference between "a building from God, an eternal house in heaven," and the spiritual body which is to be received when the last trumpet sounds (1 Cor. 15).

the Christian, for death disrobes the human spirit. So the Christian looks to the time when he will be clothed with a new body.

Second, he did not want to be without clothes (5:3). He did not want to strip off the old tent-body in death, but while still living put on the spiritual body. Whatever happened he was confident that he would not be found naked. The bodiless intermediate state was undesirable for him because the spiritual body would not have been conferred. Nevertheless during the interval between death and resurrection he would be with Christ. Not even death can separate us from the love of Christ (Rom. 8:38-39).

Third, he wanted what is mortal to be swallowed up by life (5:4). Paul was not afraid of death, but he would have been happier to be alive at the second coming of Christ. The mortal, physical frames of Christians who are alive at Christ's return will be swallowed up by life. They will be transformed and will not come into the grip of death (1 Thess. 4:15). For a Christian death is still a disruptive event and a reminder that he has not yet received full and complete deliverance. When Christ overcomes the last enemy, death, then every believer will share in the victory of life (1 Cor. 15:28).

Fourth, he was confident of receiving a new body (5:5). His assurance was that human mortality would be swallowed up by life. That kind of confidence was something he had within and he lived by it.

Paul states two reasons for such assurance. First, God had prepared him for this change.[2] He had been renewed by God's redeeming grace. Not only was this experience definite, but it also was an ongoing process—"We are being renewed day by day" (4:16). God, too, has begun a good work in us and will carry it out to completion on the day of resurrection. What assurance this should give us! The work God is doing in us now will reach its perfection on the day of Jesus Christ (Phil. 1:6). What an incentive to be faithful servants!

Second, God had given him the Holy Spirit as a guarantee (*arrabōn*, "deposit," "installment," "downpayment") of the change. The gift of the Spirit is God's pledge that He will give full and perfect life. Already we have a deposit that guarantees us this. The living presence of the Holy Spirit within guarantees us resurrection: "And if the Spirit of him who raised Jesus from the dead is living in you, he who raised Christ from the dead will also give life to your mortal bodies through his Spirit, who lives in you" (Rom. 8:11). The indwelling Holy Spirit and His daily renewal of the inward man are invincible assurance that we will be granted a new spiritual body.

---

[2]The New International Version renders *katergasamenos* in verse 5 as "has made," but it seems that "has prepared" fits the context better.

C. His Desire to Be with Christ (5:6-8)

Physical death was a possibility that Paul had to face. He did not know whether he would be among the living at the return of Christ. If he did face death, he would not become despondent. The reason was that he was full of confidence. He was confident not because he was brave but because he knew that the divine promises were sure and that God would bring him to "an eternal house in the heavens." Observe what he stressed.

1. His absence from the Lord (5:6). While Paul was in the physical body, he was away from the Lord. However, even in this life Christ really lived in him: "I no longer live, but Christ lives in me" (Gal. 2:20). The presence of Christ was real to him, but he looked for that day when he could see the risen Lord face to face. When we behold Him we can expect, as Paul did, a fuller vision of the unseen world. "Now we see but a poor reflection; then we shall see face to face. Now I know in part; then I shall know fully" (1 Cor. 13:12). As long as Paul was in his mortal body, he would not be at home with the Lord. To be sure, death would give him entrance into a fuller vision and a more intimate fellowship with the Savior. With that prospect in view Paul could face death with good courage.

2. His walk was by faith (5:7). Christ reigned in heaven and was invisible. Though Paul was "in Christ," he still lived on the earth. In this age he could not be "with Christ" in the full sense as he would when he departed. So still away from the Lord he was living by faith, not by sight.

That, too, is precisely our situation. There is a veil our eyes cannot penetrate. Our life is "now hidden with Christ in God" (Col. 3:3), but we are still citizens of the earth. This life, now hidden in Christ, is our own life, which has been radically renewed. There is no basis for this except God's mighty act of reconciliation accomplished in Christ. We know now by faith that our life is hid in Christ. It is a fact of faith; feelings are unreliable guides. Like Paul we live by faith; but with the assurance on the last day our life, now hid in Christ, will be openly and gloriously and perfectly revealed.

3. His desire to be at home with the Lord (5:8). After death Paul was certain of a "face to face" relationship with Christ. He would no longer be exiled from Christ, but at home with Him. There was a fuller life for him in heaven. He was well pleased to look forward to it. Not that he was enthusiastic about dying, but he knew that even the dead are at home with the Lord. Being there he would see his Savior more fully and be free of the failures and frustrations of the earth.

Should the Lord call on us to face death we also can be full of comfort and confidence. It is not until the end of this age that we will receive a spiritual body, but in the meantime all who fall asleep in Christ are in a joyful and blessed state. They are at home with the Lord. Their reconciliation and fellowship with Him will far exceed what we can imagine.

II. THE PROSPECT OF JUDGMENT (5:9-10)

When Christ comes again, the believer will be raised and will appear before the judgment seat of Christ. "The believer is thus always ... on his way toward the 'judgment.'"[3] The apostle Paul was not indifferent to the approaching judgment. He was conscious that he would give an account to Christ of what he had done on the earth and how effectively he had discharged his ministry of reconciliation.

A. His Aim to Be Pleasing (5:9)

He did not know whether he would be alive at the second coming or would have already departed from the body to be with the Lord. He had to leave that in the hands of God, but he had one ultimate aim in this life and in the life beyond—to please Christ. His confidence in God's reconciling grace never led him to relax his efforts to be a faithful and obedient servant.

Paul's future was in the hands of God, but such confidence had not lulled him into false security. What he said in 1 Corinthians 9:26-27 makes this clear:

I do not run like a man running aimlessly; I do not fight like a man beating the air. No, I beat my body and make it my slave so that after I have preached to others, I myself will not be disqualified for the prize.

He was committed to self-discipline and the faithful exercise of his ministry. His ambition to please the Lord prompted and inspired him in labor. Whether he was among the living or dead, or in health or sickness, or in prosperity or affliction, his desire was to so live that he would have Christ's approval. What counts is that we make every effort to please our Savior.

---

[3]Walter Künneth, *The Theology of the Resurrection*, p. 283.

B. The Certainty of His Appearance in Judgment (5:10)

On the road to Damascus Paul had been forgiven of his sins and had been reconciled to God. Nevertheless, he was destined, as all believers are, to appear before the judgment seat (*bēma*, "tribunal") of Christ. The return of Christ means judgment. It is our business to be ready. At this point we can gather together some details about the tribunal of Christ.

1. The nature of judgment. First, it is necessary (*dei*, "must," "has to"). Judgment is absolutely certain. It is according to God's purpose. It will be unavoidable and cannot be spurned. The life of every Christian must be reviewed.

Second, it is for all believers.[4] "We must all" means all of us believers. For us judgment is not something to be dreaded, but it does direct our attention to the importance of following Christ's steps and loving one another. There is no place in that kind of lifestyle for resting on spiritual accomplishments and victories of the past. It is urgent that we be diligent to exercise the ministry of reconciling people with God and people with one another. Even for Christians there is to be a day of reckoning.

Third, it is before Christ.[5] God will judge Christians through Christ. The judgment will be in the hands of Christ. On the day of judgment our present attitudes and conduct will be remembered by the One who died to heal our brokenness and to reconcile us to God.

Fourth, it is individual. It is not essentially corporate, because at that time each believer (*hekastos*, "each one") will be judged. Each individual's character and life will be brought in view. The purpose is "that each one may receive what is due him for the things done while in the body." Therefore Christ here is not viewed as judge of the life and ministry of the church as a whole but as the judge of the life and ministry of individual Christians.

Fifth, it is a judgment of work—"the things done." Every Christian will be judged on the ground of how well or poorly he has responded to God's grace. On that judgment day our Lord will know the very condition of our living as Christians. He will know if our lives were full of love and forgiveness or bitterness and hatred. He will know if we lived sacrificial or self-centered lives. He

---

[4]The final judgment of sinners will take place at the great white throne (Rev. 20:11).

[5]Paul variously identifies God or Christ as judge. The truth is that God will judge all men through Christ, as is clearly indicated by Romans 2:16: "This will take place on the day when God will judge men's secrets through Jesus Christ, as my gospel declares."

will know if we have been faithful in living the message of reconciliation and in declaring it to mankind.

Sixth, it lays open the life of every believer. "We must all appear" (*phanerōthēnai*, "be made manifest," "be completely exposed"). All disguise and pretense will be stripped away. Our personalities will be laid open as they are. Our religious hypocrisy and outward shams will be seen for what they are. Our secret motivations and thoughts will be fully exposed. The Lord "will bring to light what is hidden in darkness and will expose the motives of men's hearts" (1 Cor. 4:5). To be sure, we should never forget that our life will be laid open and will come under the penetrating gaze of Christ.

2. The results of judgment. First, the quality of conduct will be shown, whether good or bad (*phaulon*, "worthless"). Salvation is an undeserved gift, but that does not cancel our responsibility of faithfully doing God's will. The gospel must not only be received, but it also must be lived out in deeds. Grace is the foundation of the Christian life and on it we build. The building that each of us erects will be exposed to judgment. It will stand the test only if our deeds are of the character of gold, silver, and costly stones. If, on the other hand, our deeds are of the character of hay, wood, or straw, they will be judged worthless, fruitless, and thus consumed by fire (1 Cor. 3:12-15). Paul did not rule out the possibility of one who professed to be a Christian, on the basis of his lifestyle, being rejected (1 Cor. 9:27). The question for us all to ponder is what would we say should Christ ask us to explain some of our deeds when we stand before Him.

Second, each believer will receive reward for the deeds of genuine spiritual character. Grace opens to us the possibility of our doing the will of the heavenly Father. What greater incentive to good living than to hear the Lord's verdict "well done" and to receive a reward. Thus we have a compelling motive for sharing the good news of reconciliation and for building bridges where hostility, enmity, alienation, and injustice exist among men.

III. THE RECONCILING MINISTRY (5:11-21)

Having looked at the future and its consequences, Paul focused next on God's reconciling grace through Christ and our responsibilities before God and men.

A. The Motives for Ministry (5:11-14a)

It has been made clear that we are to be judged by our deeds. Paul lived and served with a consciousness he was on his way to the judgment. Before the judgment seat of Christ his own ministry, which had been marked by unselfish service and integrity, would be reviewed. He was confident, but with the prospect of judgment his confidence gave him no carefree ease.

1. He persuaded men because of the "fear of the Lord" (5:11).   His fear was due to the fact that his motives and Christian service are to be inspected at the judgment seat of Christ. The full awareness that he must stand before the divine Lord prompted him to persuade men to accept the message of reconciliation. He wanted no blood on his hands. So he gave himself tirelessly to evangelism and soul-winning.

The judgment was sobering, but he was reassured that it was plain to God what he was. He was convinced that God would approve his life and ministry. Nevertheless the apostle had a deep reverential fear of what was to come. Is there anything for a Christian to fear in God? There is. He should fear the consequences of a misspent life. He should fear the examination of Christ if his service is hypocritical and selfish.

2. He had only pure motives (5:12-13).   The Corinthians had reason for being proud of Paul. It was not that he was guilty of egotistical boasting, but they could be proud that his life was free of any blame. He was a faithful and sincere servant of the gospel. Whatever he did was "for the sake of God" and for the sake of the Corinthians. If he were beside himself at times because of extraordinary spiritual experiences (12:1-4), that was no sign he was insane. Such experiences were due to the inspiration of the Holy Spirit, and they were "for the sake of God"—precious times of close communion and conversation with God. These experiences were infrequent, and he had not used them to impress others. His private spiritual experiences were precious, but he did not get lost in them so that he was no earthly good. He knew where his responsibility lay and had not neglected his ministry. There is a temptation to become so absorbed in divine mysteries that bearing the cross has little, if any, place in our experience. An even greater temptation is to preen ourselves as being superior to other Christians because God granted to us visions and revelations.

3. He was controlled by Christ's love[6] (5:14a).   Christ's powerful love for Paul

---

[6]The New International Version translates the phrase "the love of Christ" as a subjective genitive—"Christ's love for us," but it can be rendered as an objective genitive—"our love for Christ." Paul's thought must be "Christ's love for us." This provides a suitable introduction to what follows in verses 14b-21.

controlled him, not against his will but "because we are convinced," he said, "that one died for all." What a profound understanding of the cross! Christ's love for lost and dying men and women is proven by His death (Rom. 5:8; Gal. 2:20). Christ's love set in motion Paul's love for Him and drove him to a life of service. It impelled him to abandon his selfish pursuits and to devote himself to the message: God provides healing for the broken world through the cross. It is the love of Christ that constrains us to a life that is pleasing to God. Our response to the great outpouring of love through the cross is seen in the extent to which we live for Christ.

B. The Death of Christ (5:14-17)

At the cross is precisely where the ministry of reconciliation began. The Father used the cross of His Son as the means to bring new, reconciled life. The suffering of the Son of God is reconciling suffering; His death is an atoning sacrifice.

1. Christ died for all (5:14b-15a).   The crucifixion was for mankind as a whole. Christ died in their place *(huper)* and for their benefit. "One died for all, and therefore all died." What is the meaning of "all died"? All men are potentially dead in Christ. When one comes to Christ, he dies out to sin and death. So he dies to the old life and is raised to "live a new life" (Rom. 6:1-11). The new life is a life with new aims and purposes.

2. Christ died that the living might die to themselves and live for Him (5:15b).   His death was not merely to deliver us from sin and judgment. The cross of Christ was so that we may live—not for ourselves but for Him. The same love and spirit of sacrifice that prompted Him to die should become more and more evident in us as we continue in fellowship with Him. This is what qualifies us to take the needs of men seriously and to be genuine agents of reconciliation.

3. All things are new in Christ (5:16-17).   Dying to self and living for Christ had two consequences for Paul.

The first was a new knowledge. His experiences on the Damascus road gave him a new view of life, especially of Jesus Christ. Before he realized that Christ's death wipes away our sin, he regarded Him as well as His associates "from a worldly point of view." To put it more literally, he once knew Christ only "according to the flesh" *(kata sarka)*, that is, according to outward appearance, as a renegade Jew and revolutionary rabbi who, as he thought, had been rightly crucified. But all this had been changed: "Though we once regarded

Christ in this way, we do so no longer." His knowledge of Christ was transformed when he met the ever-living Christ who dwelt among men and who now dwells in the hearts of believers.

When he encountered Jesus as Savior, he received a new knowledge, a fuller understanding of Christ. He acknowledged Him as Lord (Acts 9:4-11). We, too, need to know Him as Lord, the Supreme Reconciler, who wills to reconcile all men to God as He did Paul. Really knowing Him should prompt us to live a confessional life—confessing Christ daily as Lord.

The second consequence was a new creation (5:17). Jesus did not bring a new religion but a new creation. As was Paul, every Christian is a new creation. "The old has gone, the new has come." All of this is "in Christ." Just as at creation chaos gave way to order and darkness to light, so the Christian has passed from the evil age of darkness to that of light. The Christian lives in a new order. He himself is a new creation, a new man, being transformed into the likeness of Christ with ever-increasing glory (3:18). There is a great change—a sharp reorientation of our loyalties, new hopes, new joys. There is a new lifestyle determined by the fact that we are in Christ. There is a new order of relationships at work between God and us and between us and our fellow man. These really do change everything. To live in Christ is to be a new creation, in a right relationship with both God and man.

C. The Work of God (5:18-21)

All that was involved in this mighty change—the new knowledge and the new creation—was from God. It was all God's glorious redemptive work. He took the initiative.

1. God reconciled Paul and others (5:18). There was no way they could have done that for themselves. God took a decisive step in Christ to bridge the gulf between Himself and mankind. All people were alienated from God and undeserving of divine favor, but He brought into personal fellowship with Himself those who came to faith in Christ. One summary of the great plan of salvation can be put in three sentences, which read like this:

God created men in fellowship with Him.
Man broke fellowship.
God restored fellowship, through Christ.

Through a personal experience with Christ we find ourselves at one with God. Through Christ we are called to peace, to unity, to new bonds of fellowship.

2. God reconciled the world (5:19a). Man cannot overcome the power of sin and his estrangement from his Creator. He cannot change himself from a self-centered to a God-loving and neighbor-loving person. God in His power and goodness stepped in to heal the estrangement and to reconcile us to Himself. This profound truth is expressed in the words: "God was reconciling the world to himself in Christ, not counting men's sins against them."

Here is the heart of the gospel: (1) The initiative was with God; He bridged the chasm of estrangement created by our sin and rebellion. (2) The mediator was Christ; He stood between God and man and brought us into fellowship. Reconciliation centers in the cross-death in which Christ satisfied the broken law of God and took the penalty of sin in our stead. By dying He stood in the breach for us. (3) The result was the blotting out of the guilt of sin. No longer does God count (*logizomai*, "reckon," "impute") our sins against us. From His point of view, our sins have been blotted out as if they had never been. This does not mean that the results of sin are annulled. If we ruin our health, it is likely we will have to live with the consequences. The fact that God does not any longer count sins against us means that God opened the way to reconciliation. Men can receive it—the gift of peace with God.

3. God committed the message of reconciliation to men (5:19b-20). To men God has given the ministry of handing on the message (*logos*, "word") of reconciliation. The whole Church—redeemed, forgiven, reconciled, Spirit-empowered—is obligated to this ministry. This is every Christian's ministry. It belongs to all and not just to some.

God has now entrusted to us the good news that the world is reconciled. So we are ambassadors for Christ. The Savior is the chief ambassador, but He has delegated us as messengers of peace. He stood in our stead. Now we stand in for Him. But what is our message? "Be ye reconciled to God." Would that we had the courage to make this appeal to everyone we meet. God offers reconciliation, but it can not be complete unless men accept this message. Men need to hear the heralds of the cross.

4. The death of Christ is the heart of reconciliation (5:21). At the cross reconciliation on God's side was completed. There our sin was imputed to Christ: "God made him who had no sin to be sin for us." This means that Christ bore away the sin of the world and its penalty. He shared in our condition—"the likeness of sinful man" (Rom. 8:3), but sin had no place in Him. Guilt issuing from our transgressions was placed to His account. Christ took our place, estranged from God and the object of divine wrath.

The end of redemptive work is that "we might become the righteousness of God." That is, through faith Christ's righteousness is imputed to us. We are acquitted of sin and reconciled. No longer are we God's enemies, but His friends. Christ is our peace. Through His life, death, and resurrection He broke down the dividing walls of sin and hatred that alienate us from God and from one another.

IV. CONCLUSION

The true servant of Jesus Christ performs a ministry of reconciliation. The dynamic motivation of this ministry is twofold. One is the prospect of glorification and standing before Jesus Christ in judgment. The other is God's outpouring of His love through the reconciling death of His Son on the cross. The touchstone of the Christian ministry is Christ's death in our behalf. Paul wrote: "God demonstrates his own love for us in this: While we were still sinners, Christ died for us" (Rom. 5:8). These wonderful words mean precisely what they say. The fact remains that the One who loved us so much is the One before whom we will stand in the day of judgment.

In light of Christ's love and the coming judgment we should be diligent to exercise the ministry of reconciliation which God has entrusted to all His people. This ministry can be described in the following dimensions:

(1) The divine initiative: "God was reconciling the world to himself in Christ, not counting men's sins against them."

(2) The human response: the new creation, the call to be reconciled and the call to be Christ's ambassadors.

(3) The scope: "the world"—men of all nations, all generations, all groups and all classes.

God has committed this great program of service to all Christians of every time and every place. So much depends upon this ministry because it is so vast and far-reaching. Christ came to bear away the world's sins (John 1:29). He came to make reconciliation between the world and God. God lays on us a ministry which covers all men of all centuries. All men need to hear what Christ has done for them so that they, too, may have the opportunity to participate in the reconciling work of Christ and thus to take up the work of the ministry.

Participation in the work of the ministry means that Christians cannot be content with their life in the local church so long as there are still human beings who have never heard of Christ. The ministry of reconciliation is for the whole of humanity. In no generation have all the inhabitants of the earth been given the opportunity to hear the gospel of Christ.

The church's vision and outreach have seldom been more than a token participation in the Lord's ministry of the world's salvation. The scope of the ministry is restricted when the church turns in upon itself and becomes preoccupied with administration and internal action in which the task of evangelizing the world and of practical service may be incidental. Internal squabblings, strife, and power plays in denominations and local churches have diverted energies that should have gone into efforts to strengthen the church spiritually and into home and foreign missions. Racial tensions in and outside the church have hampered the outreach of the gospel. The indifference and the indolence of the many have sapped the vitality of the church and impeded the zealous efforts of the few. "It is time for judgment to begin with the family of God" (1 Peter 4:17).

If the ministry of reconciliation is accomplished, there must be a ministry to the world. Do we disqualify ourselves of an effective exercise of this ministry by rivalry and quarrelsome disputes and coldness and selfishness and pride? The eternal reach of ministry should drive us to lay aside every hindrance to our call to serve. An awareness that this is an eternal ministry adds to our sense of unworthiness and insufficiency, but we need not faint. Indwelt by the Holy Spirit, we are encouraged and empowered to fulfill our ministry of reconciliation. Conscious that we are called to the privilege of an eternal ministry, it is urgent that we take up the task of reconciling men to God. It is before Christ who loved us and gave Himself for us that we will stand and give an account for this ministry: "God was reconciling the world to himself in Christ ... and he committed to us the message of reconciliation" (5:19).

6

The Christian and His Relationships

2 Corinthians 6:1—7:1

Christianity is a religion of relationships. Christ so identified Himself with us fallen men that He took the burden of our sin and guilt. Through His death He built a bridge between God and men and between men and men. This reconciling mission was not and could not have been accomplished by His remaining aloof. He became involved. He entered into our situation and stood in our place. He shared our lot. What He did made it possible for us to enter into fellowship with God.

The apostle Paul was inspired by the example of his Lord. Fruitful relationships were vital to his transmission of the message of reconciliation. He sought to build trust-relationships and to identify with those whom he served. Having the confidence of others was crucial to his ministry. God did help him; but God worked through Paul's efforts, as He does ours, to establish relationships with others. Consequently Paul sought to give no offense to the church and to commend himself to the world by his exemplary conduct.

Paul's purpose was to promote the fellowship of the saints, but at the same time he was concerned about the relationship of the church to the world. "The Christian community always has been subject to temptation in two opposite directions in its relation to the world: either to flee the world and to be separate from it or to embrace the world and to become absorbed by it."[1] Paul insisted

---

[1]Arnold B. Come, *Agents of Reconciliation*, p. 13.

on the separation so that the church at Corinth would not become infected with the sins of the world, relax its discipline, and lose its identity by accommodation to the world. For him separation from the world was not isolation from it. His conviction was that Christ is not only the Savior of the world, but that every Christian is an agent in the ministry of reconciliation. The church, therefore, must be concerned about the life of the world as well as with its own life. In its own life it is a holy fellowship, a fellowship "in Christ," but the church must move toward the outside world to fulfill its commission to go forth as a witness "to the ends of the earth" (Acts 1:8).

In his Christian service Paul sought to establish and maintain good relations. He urged the Christian community to preserve its purity and holiness of life while building bridges to unbelievers and beseeching them to be reconciled to God.

I. AN ENDEAVOR TO GIVE NO OFFENSE (6:1-10)

There is strength in fellowship. Through his communion with God Paul became a channel of God's power, an agent of reconciliation. God's grace was free, but that did not set aside the need for human decision and perseverance. He urged his readers to accept and hold fast to the message of reconciliation; but he did it with care, attempting to avoid putting obstacles in their way.

A. In His Plea to the Church (6:1-2)

Above all Paul desired to be a minister of reconciliation. That caused him to endure great hardships and labor tirelessly in the gospel. He strived constantly to be a channel of God's reconciling love to men and to avoid an occasion for anyone to take offense at what he did. His urgent appeal to the Corinthians was completely in harmony with his ministry, and it made clear his love for them.

1. The basis of the plea (6:1a, 2). It was twofold. First, he was one of "God's fellow workers." His Christian service was an active partnership with God. He was not a religious super star nor was he running his own religious show. He was God's agent, however, not merely working for Him but working with Him. What a privilege it is to work with God! What an honored place and true joy! Every Christian has been called to the greatest and most honorable work in all the world—a work in which we are laborers together with God—a work in which we are partners with God. "We are therefore Christ's ambassadors, as though God were making his appeal through us" (5:20). Working with God, we are to be committed to the ministry of the evangelical entreaty: "Be reconciled to God."

Second, "Now is the day of salvation." The day of reconciliation had dawned through the death and resurrection of Christ. Since the coming of Christ, God has been waiting to accept men, to restore them to Himself. "Now is the time of God's favor." Now is God's time for reconciliation. The period from the cross to the end is the time of decision that shapes men's destiny. Every day in this period is tense with urgency and filled with the possibilities that open the way to eternal life. Men and women are called to decision by the word of reconciliation. All that is needed is for them to accept God's offer of saving grace. For people to pass up this tremendous opportunity is a tragic thing. They choose to remain alienated from God rather than to be reconciled. They desire to be slaves of sin rather than to be liberated. They continue in their brokenness rather than to be restored and healed by God's grace. None of these people should be marked off. They are in desperate spiritual need. The ambassador of Christ should not be slack in building bridges to them and in carrying to them the good news of reconciliation.

2. The purpose of the plea: "not to receive God's grace in vain" (6:1b).   Christ had died for the Corinthians. They had believed on Christ. They were to cease to live for themselves and from henceforth to live for Him (5:15). If they failed to do this, then Paul's concern was that God's grace bestowed on them was in vain. Grace provided for their reconciliation and a life which Paul described as a "new creation" (5:17). So they received God's free favor, but the peril was that they would fail now to show that the old things had passed away and new things had come. The gospel must be lived and shared with others. Whoever fails to conform his life to it and to be concerned about his work as a reconciler among men is receiving God's grace in vain.

B. In His Ministry to the Church (6:3)

Paul made his plea to the Corinthian church, but there was still another matter that concerned him—the importance of personal behavior and relationships. This should be a concern of every believer and has both a negative and positive side.

1. To avoid putting a stumbling block in anyone's path.   The apostle was careful not to give offense. Of course he had principles by which he lived. He contended for the faith and was not a "wishy-washy" person who kept peace at any price. However, he sought to maintain good interpersonal relations with other believers. He did it not to avoid personal censure. What mattered was his ministry. He was careful to do nothing that would discredit it. If there were those who refused to accept the message of God's reconciling love, it would not be because Paul had put a stumbling block in their way. He attempted to avoid giving any offense which would give men and women an excuse to close their hearts to the gospel of reconciliation. More than anything Paul desired to see others walk again with their Maker. As true reconcilers we, too, must take every precaution not to put obstacles in anyone's path. Our conduct is a vital factor in ministry. Unfortunate experiences and disappointments with servants of Christ have put unnecessary obstacles in the way of some people.

2. To show[2] himself to be God's servant.   How did he demonstrate that he was a servant of God? By praise of himself? By ambition? By being over-bearing? By being a superspiritual? By ruthlessness? No! He did it by purity of motives, by purity of conduct, and by a willingness to suffer for Jesus' sake. His only ambition and passion was to be found a faithful servant of God. Like his Lord he came to serve, not to be served. That was exactly what he wanted his Corinthian friends to understand. Among them he had shown himself to be devoted to a life of ministry and service. Every Christian is called to live in the service of Christ.

C. In His Conduct Before the Church and World (6:4-10)

As God's servant Paul experienced many hardships and adversities. It comes as no surprise that he wrote: "I bear on my body the marks of Jesus" (Gal. 6:17). His life in Christ included the wonderful ministry of reconciliation and the price of discipleship. He never sought, as many do, Christianity without a cross. In every way he showed himself to be a servant of God. His experiences were manifold and can be divided as follows: outward adversities, response to God's grace, work of preaching the gospel, and paradoxes of his ministry.

1. His outward adversities (6:5).   While care must be taken not to overpress the distinctions in this "catalog of adversities," they do fall into three different

---

[2]The participle *(sunistanontes)* is present, indicating that Paul made it a common practice of showing himself to be God's servant. Some scholars prefer rendering this participle here "commend" rather than "show."

groups. The first group refers to pressures (troubles, hardships, distresses). *Troubles* (*thlipsis*) is a general term for distressing trials. On his final visit to Jerusalem Paul knew what would befall him there. In bidding the Ephesian elders farewell he reminded them that the Holy Spirit had warned him that he would face prison and troubles (*thlipsis*) in the Holy City (Acts 20:23). The apostle was fully confident that troubles could not separate a believer from the love of Christ (Rom. 8:35).

The word *hardships* (*anankais*) generally means "necessities," but the context here requires "hardships" or "trials" that are unavoidable. Paul found himself in circumstances in which hardships could not be avoided. No doubt he had in view such suffering when he wrote: "We are hard pressed on every side, but not crushed; perplexed, but not in despair" (2 Cor. 4:8).

The concept *distresses (stenochōriais)* literally means "straits." The picture is a narrow place with no way of escape. These are experiences that are compressing, confining, and perplexing. God's children can be assured that He will provide a way out (1 Cor. 10:13). Christians are able to rejoice in troubles, hardships, and distresses provided they are borne for Christ's sake.[3]

The second group of adversities concerns persecutions (beatings, imprisonments, riots). The apostle endured terrible beatings (*plēgais*, "stripes," "lashes"). On five different occasions he received from the Jews forty lashes minus one (11:24). This particular kind of suffering may be removed from our experience, but many of the early Christians knew what it was to be beaten with rods and flogged. Paul also endured the indignity of imprisonments (*phulakais*). He wrote: "I ... have ... been in prison more frequently" (11:23). One such instance is in Acts 16:23f., where we are told that he was flogged, thrown into prison, and his feet were placed in stocks. Furthermore, he was a victim of riots (*akatastasiais*, "mob violence"). Many of the Jews hated Paul with a passion. They did not spare any efforts to inflame the street mobs against him (Acts 13:50; 14:5, 19; 16:22; 17:5; 18:12; 21:27f.).

The third group of hardships refers to ministerial burdens (hard work, sleepless nights, hunger). The pressures and persecutions that Paul endured were imposed from without. Frequently they were the result of the animosity of men. On the other hand, his ministry of reconciliation also made it necessary for him to endure willingly certain burdens, one of which was hard work (*kopois*). This could have included both his labors for Christ in the gospel and manual labor to earn his daily bread. He plied his trade as a tentmaker so that

---

[3]Philip E. Hughes, *The Second Epistle to the Corinthians* (The New International Commentary on the New Testament), p. 224.

he would not be a burden especially to the Corinthian church (11:7, 9, 10; 1 Cor. 9:12, 15). The apostle spent himself for the gospel and knew weariness in mind and body.

Moreover, Paul voluntarily went without sleep (agrupniais, "watchings"), but less rest allowed him to devote more time to his evangelistic work. He did not suffer from insomnia. Many of his sleepless nights were due to his care and concern for all of the churches. He was deeply perplexed at times by the problems that the young churches faced, and he agonized in prayer on their behalf.

In addition, Paul willingly endured hunger so that others might hear of God's efforts to reconcile errant mankind. He was ready to make the necessary sacrifices for the gospel. "I have learned," he said, "the secret of being content in any and every situation, whether well-fed or hungry, whether living in plenty or in want" (Phil. 4:12).

Paul had no "martyr's complex." He did not seek out trouble, difficulty, and afflictions. It was his experience to suffer for Jesus' sake. For him cross-bearing was inseparable from the ministry of reconciliation. The temptation is real today to think that when something is not pleasurable or it fails to produce happiness that it is not good. Everything is assessed in terms of the principle of pleasure. Servants of Christ cannot evade the cross. Self-denial is an integral part of the ministry God has committed to every Christian. We are called to share in the cross.

2. His response to God's grace (6:6-7a). The ministry of reconciliation involved Paul in struggles, conflicts and tribulations. Yet, at the same time, there was the undergirding strength from God enabling him to endure all these bitter experiences. He listed several spiritual graces that marked his ministry. The first is purity (hagnotēti). This is a reference to his life in general—his motives, his desires, and his conduct. All these were pure. It is only wisdom for a Christian to be pure in thought, word, and deed so that offense will not be given.

The second spiritual grace is understanding (gnōsei, "knowledge"). The knowledge that Paul possessed was God's truth as it is in Jesus Christ. He understood the Christian message, and his letters are a wealth of spiritual insight. A servant of Christ should be acquainted with a wide range of subjects, but he especially should know the Bible. This Book speaks to our wounded and unhealed feelings and holds out hope for those who are alienated from the household of faith. The message of the Bible is what the church and the world need to hear and understand.

The third spiritual grace is patience (makrothumiai, "longsuffering"). This is manifested under ill-treatment. Indignities had been inflicted on Paul (6:4, 5), but these called for the exercise of longsuffering. It is the refusal to be provoked. It is the refusal to be hasty in speech. Uncontrolled feelings and words can add fuel to a dangerous flame. Longsuffering is a grace that is a universal need.

The fourth spiritual grace is kindness (*chrēstotēti*). It does not really need to be defined. It can take people out of the grip of this cold, impersonal, self-seeking world. It can melt the indifference of men and women to our message. Christian kindness is an effective way to introduce the good news of reconciliation. Preaching and teaching are important, but little deeds of kindness are also used by God to touch people's lives so that He may heal their brokenness.

The fifth is the Holy Spirit *(pneuma hagion)*. It is somewhat surprising that Paul included the Holy Spirit in a list of spiritual graces.[4] However, it is credible since spiritual graces are the fruit and blessing of the Holy Spirit (Gal. 5:22-23). Through a vital relationship with the Holy Spirit, Paul was able to bear hardships. The indwelling Holy Spirit produces spiritual wholeness and holiness of life. He imparts power for Christian service.

The sixth spiritual grace is sincere love (*agapēi*, "unhypocritical love"). Genuine love is the primary fruit of the Holy Spirit. It is more than kindness, which can be shown for the sake of courtesy. Love calls for a personal interest in people. It values people as individuals and seeks their good. No doubt, differences exist among believers in any church. Feuds, factions, and fusses crop up in church, but pure love reconciles and binds together those who are in Christ. Fellowship and fervent love among God's people far exceed discord and friction.

The seventh grace is truthful speech *(logōi alētheias)*.[5] People need to have complete confidence in what we say and to know that our statements can be trusted. Being strictly honest is the rule in telling others about God's reconciling grace and what it means to us. Exaggeration has no place in Christian witnessing. Truthful speech is vital to fellowship and fruitful relationships. When the words of men are deemed unreliable, communications break down. Jesus Himself was emphatic about the importance of the truthfulness of our words: "I tell you that men will have to give account on the day of judgment for every careless word they have spoken. For by your words you will be acquitted, and by your words you will be condemned" (Matt. 12:36-37).

---

[4]Some biblical scholars assume that in this verse "spirit" is the human spirit and holy is the description of an ethical quality. According to this view it should be translated "a spirit which is holy" and be understood to distinguish a true servant of God from a false one.

[5]The phrase may be translated "the word of truth" which is the gospel (Col. 1:5; James 1:18), that is, the message Paul proclaimed. The reference, however, may be to the truthfulness of his words.

The last spiritual grace is the power of God (*dunamei theou*). Paul had seen the power of God at work in his ministry. He reminded his converts at Corinth of this fact in an earlier letter to them: "I came to you in weakness and fear, and with much trembling. My message and my preaching were not with wise and persuasive words, but with a demonstration of the Spirit's power, so that your faith might not rest on men's wisdom, but on God's power" (1 Cor. 2:3-5). It was the powerful work of the Holy Spirit that convicted the Corinthians of their sin and brought them into fellowship with God. There was no church in Corinth when Paul first visited the city. The church there was a new creation, and every member of it was a new creation. The existence of that church was evidence of God's mighty power. His power works today in human hearts, homes, businesses, and churches, reconciling men and women to Himself and healing human relationships.

3. His work of declaring the gospel (6:7b).   As a minister of the gospel Paul was a soldier of Christ. He was engaged in conflict with the powers of darkness. He reminded his readers of two facts relevant to this conflict. First, his weapon was righteousness. He employed no carnal means to accomplish his ends. Later he wrote: "The weapons we fight with are not the weapons of the world. On the contrary, they have divine power to tear down strongholds" (10:4). Spiritual warfare must be waged with spiritual weapons. Paul's only weapon was his righteousness, which clearly indicates that Christians must always do the right. Where there have been conflicts among Christians some have resorted to using carnal means in the attempt to achieve spiritual ends. Spiritual warfare cannot be prosecuted successfully by the use of unworthy means.

Second, his equipment was complete. He had "weapons of righteousness in his right hand and in his left." That kind of armor prepared him for any attack. Conflict with the enemy of our souls is unavoidable, but God has sufficiently equipped us to withstand his assaults.

4. The paradoxes of his ministry (6:8-10).   Having described the spiritual qualities of his ministry, Paul went on to speak of the twofold response that he encountered. Christian experience has its paradoxes. These are difficult, if not impossible, to understand and reconcile. Paul shared the same paradoxes of humiliation and glory as did his Lord. These of which he spoke we can classify in terms of four areas of his experience.

The first was a matter of reputation. Some honored him and held him in esteem while others held him in dishonor. One met him with praise; another blamed and condemned him. Some saw him as being genuine and sincere, but others viewed him as an imposter and deceiver. For some he was an unknown, a nobody, who supposedly lacked the credentials of a true apostle (3:1). Negative human assessment did not affect his commitment to the ministry of reconciliation. If we are judged by the values of the world we, too, may be held in ill repute, accused of being imposters, and seen as nobodies. The truth is that many have enjoyed a far wider reputation through knowing Christ and through being faithful to the discharge of their ministry. Zaccheus, Paul, Augustine, John Knox, and scores of others are examples.

The second paradox was a matter of health. This is stated in the words: "dying and yet we live on; beaten and yet not killed." Paul did not lead a sheltered life, for he carried with him the death of Jesus and death was at work in him (4:10, 12). He lived in the midst of danger, under constant adversity and peril (11:23f.; 1 Cor. 15:30f.; Acts 14:19f.). He even saw his "thorn in the flesh" as serving a worthwhile purpose. To keep him from becoming conceited because of great revelations he had received, the Lord refused to take it away (12:7-9). But God delivered him from suffering and dangers that would have proved fatal. He lived dangerously but also gloriously. Christians are called to live the same way. To do this involves bringing men and women face to face with the gospel and exposing their hurts to the healing graces of God, regardless of what it costs in ridicule, oppression, and suffering.

The third paradox was a matter of mental state. Paul was "sorrowful, yet always rejoicing." Like his Lord, he was "a man of sorrows and acquainted with grief" (Isa. 53:3). Because of the conditions at Corinth he had written a letter to the Christians out of much anguish of hurt and many tears (2:4). He told his friends at Philippi that God had spared him of "sorrow on sorrows" by restoring Epaphroditus to health (Phil. 2:27). There is no doubt he had his full measure of grief, but that did not make him callous. He remained sensitive to the pain and hurt of others. He urged his readers to "mourn with those who mourn" (Rom. 12:15). Sorrows and troubles did not quench his joy (7:4, 7, 9; 13:9; Rom. 12:12, 15; 14:17).

Sorrow and joy belong together in the Christian experience. This springs from sharing in Christ's suffering and in the power of his resurrection (Phil. 3:10). Sorrows can drive a man to despair, but they make us who have been reconciled to God reach out and lay hold on Christ with a firmer grip. In the midst of sorrows we can always have the joy of reconciliation and the assurance of victory. Therefore the clarion call is "Rejoice in the Lord always. I will say it again: Rejoice!" (Phil. 4:4). Such joy has a way of turning people on to the gospel.

The fourth paradox was a matter of finance. The picture here is that of destruction—"poor, yet making many rich; having nothing and yet possessing everything." Paul did not despise wealth. He did not claim any virtue or merit in his poverty in the world's goods. Only to the poverty of the Son of God have virtue and merit been attached. The Son of God voluntarily became poor for our sakes. At the heart of the message of reconciliation lies this wonderful truth: "Though he was rich, yet for our sakes he became poor, so that you through his poverty might become rich" (8:9). Christ is the "pearl of great price"—the wealth of the Christian—an everlasting enrichment.

Outside of Jesus Christ, Paul possessed nothing nor does anyone. The ones who buy in this age do not really possess what they purchase. When the new age completely dawns, an end will be put to such ownership. That is what Paul meant by "having nothing." Man in this age possesses nothing unless he has an inheritance in the age to come. Through Christ alone is the lordship which Adam lost restored to mankind. For the Corinthians that was a fact. Paul reminded them earlier: "...all things are yours, and you are of Christ..." (1 Cor. 3:22,23). "You are of Christ" meant they belonged to Him. They had been bought at an infinite price (1 Cor. 6:19f.), and thus were not their own. Nevertheless they possessed everything, not by their own right but by their position in Christ. The magnitude of God's act of giving His Son assures us that He will "graciously give us all things" (Rom. 8:32).

We may have a superabundance of the material things of life, but we do not possess them. We came into the world empty-handed, and we will leave the same way (1 Tim. 6:7). What we possess in Christ we will possess forever. Through God's reconciling grace we have been restored to wholeness in Jesus Christ, and granted an eternal inheritance—"treasures in heaven, where moth and rust do not destroy and where thieves do not break in and steal" (Matt. 6:20).

II. SEPARATION AND HOLINESS (6:11—7:1)

To the Corinthians Paul had spoken freely and had poured his heart out. He lowered the barriers and revealed his innermost thoughts and the great love he had for them. He knew that the shaping of reconciling attitudes involved hard and long work. The truth is that relationships cannot be programmed; but as Paul did at Corinth, we need to put forth the effort to construct trust-relationships. Consider Paul's effort to reconcile the Corinthians.

A. Their Separation from Him (6:11-13)

Conflict can be suppressed. When it is, pressure builds. If it is not abated, there will be a large explosion. Paul must have known this. He did not fear conflict as a "no-no," nor did he seek to create it. When conflict did arise, he set about to right the situation and to extinguish the smoldering fire. That is what he sought to do in dealing with the Corinthians who were estranged. He recognized that their feelings toward him could become a conflagration of bitterness and deep alienation. His effort was to establish and maintain good personal relationships with them.

1. His love for them (6:11). The apostle was not cool toward the Corinthians. He did not hold back his affection, and had not been afraid to express his feelings, even though he could have been hurt and disappointed by them. That was a risk, but he was willing to take it. He opened wide his heart to them and gave them a permanent place in his affections. Genuine, undiluted love will always work. It breaks down barriers that separate men and bridges gaps between them. For this to occur Christians must not only talk about love but must be infected with it.

2. Their alienation from him (6:12). The Corinthians had been cold toward Paul. Any barrier or cold feeling of separation was due to their response. He had taken a very significant step—opening his heart to them. It was not likely that he expected a dramatic, sudden solution; but the Corinthians were still cautious, holding back their affections. They were unjustly suspicious and unwilling to call off their hostilities against Paul. They squeezed him out of their hearts and gave him little place in their love. Dealing with the estrangement of those people was not easy. Paul's desire was to build a trust-relationship between himself and them, but building such a relationship is never easy where distrust exists.

3. His call for them to reciprocate (6:13). The apostle urged his spiritual children at Corinth to put away unjust suspicion. He had freely poured out his affection on them. He asked for a like response from them. Separation and alienation were from their side, not from his. The ministry of reconciliation was at work. Paul had seen to that, but for it to be completed the Corinthians needed to commit themselves fully to being Christians and to lay aside suspicion or prejudice that impeded their fellowship with the apostle.

As Paul well knew, personal hurts, distrust, and malice ruin relationships. Because these are difficult to cope with, some churches have become resigned to estrangements. In many instances families in the same church need to be reconciled to one another. Between them have been longstanding fusses, feuds, and strife. When their estrangement surfaces, the fellowship of the local church is disrupted. Moreover, in the midst of many individual families alienation exists. Where the so-called "generation gap" exists, the home atmosphere is strained and there is little communication and love between parents and children. There are husbands and wives who have lived together for years, but they have not learned how to talk and share.

Many of us may live in alienation. The ministry of reconciliation is needed. Through this ministry we can become out and out Christians and experience God's reconciling love at all levels of our existence. That opens wide our hearts to others and to their needs. The reality of this experience is expressed in a lifestyle of fellowship. Mutual love is the basis for fruitful relationships in the home, in the church, and in all of life. By God's grace and our diligence we can construct such relationships.

B. Their Fellowship with Unbelievers (6:14-18)

The plea had been made for the Corinthians to open their hearts to Paul as his had been opened to them. For them to turn to God and to him, God's servant, they would have to break with the world. Being aware of that, Paul emphasized the importance of their not becoming infected with the sins of the broken world.

1. Argument for separation (6:14-16a). The apostle admonished the believers at Corinth to open wide their hearts to him, but he also gave a warning: "Do not be yoked together with unbelievers."[6] This does not mean that a believer must keep aloof from unbelievers or reject them but that he should not form ties that put him in a compromising position. Pagan influences were a threat, but necessary business relations and friendliness with unbelievers were not prohibited. To be an effective minister of reconciliation the Christian must have interest in the unsaved and treat them with understanding. Paul warned the Corinthian Christians to shun associations and people that would turn them away from the Christian way of life. God has not taken the community of faith out of the world, but He sent it to the world. While living and serving in the

---

[6]In the back of Paul's mind must have been Deuteronomy 22:10: "Do not plow an ox and a donkey yoked together." This teaches that some things are fundamentally incompatible.

world the members must keep a prophetic distance. Without such a distance the church runs the risk of becoming worldly.

There was just cause for the apostolic injunction: "Do not be yoked together with unbelievers." This was consistent with what Paul said about the relationship of Christians with unbelievers elsewhere. In light of what he wrote in 1 Corinthians three observations are noteworthy here. (1) The Christian was not expected to withdraw from the world and have no contact with sinners, but he was not to associate with those in the church guilty of immoral conduct (1 Cor. 5:9-11). (2) Paul did not expect the breaking up of a marriage in which only one of the partners had become a Christian (1 Cor. 7:12-16). Such a marriage was not to be dissolved unless the unbeliever insisted on it. However, when a widow remarried, she was to choose a Christian (1 Cor. 7:39). This makes clear that Paul had strong reservations about any Christian's marrying an unbeliever. Complete harmony is impossible when only one of the partners has been born again. (3) Christians were not asked to abstain from dinner parties given by unbelievers, though Paul was aware that this could create a problem (1 Cor. 10:27-33).

Christians were to have the distinction of being "in the world yet not of it." They were to live in the midst of unbelievers and have contact with them, hoping to reconcile them to God.[7] However, the church must be on guard so that the world does not squeeze the church into its mold. Christians need to remind themselves that they are members of the holy people and are consecrated to God's service (1 Cor. 1:2; 3:16-17; Rom. 1:7).

It is urgent for the church today, as it was for the one at Corinth, to make up its mind about the importance of its purity. The church must first minister to its own needs before it can reach out into the community and minister to the needs there. The church has often lost its zest for purity and has made peace with the world in exchange for comfort, power, and prestige. This is not the reconciliation of the world but a capitulation to mammon. Fundamentally the church is incompatible with the values and lifestyle of the world.

Expounding this fact, Paul raised a sequence of five questions:

(1) "What do righteousness and wickedness have in common?" (*metochē*, "partnership," "sharing"). This focuses on the broad range of contacts between Christians and unbelievers. Can deep partnership and intimate sharing exist between the two? They are separated by their opposite reactions to the gospel. The righteousness of Christians has nothing in common with the wickedness (*anomia*, "lawlessness") of unbelievers. Because of this it is often

---

[7] 1 Cor. 7:16 is a special example.

necessary for Christians to make a clear break with old associates. Christians, however, must guard against two dangers, one of which is self-righteousness. A self-righteous, superior attitude causes people to despise us and because of us the Savior whom we profess. The other danger is an excessive preoccupation with our own soul's welfare. When we become overly engrossed in our spirituality, we lead a self-centered life in which no place is given to the ministry of reconciliation.

(2) "What fellowship can light have with darkness?" Those who are habitual evildoers and who refuse the light of the gospel have no place in the Christian fellowship. As a last resort Jesus Himself said that an obstinate evildoer must be treated as a heathen and a publican (Matt. 18:15-17, cf. 1 Cor. 5:1-5). The church must be concerned about its purity. Otherwise it cannot be God's instrument of service in the world. Therefore any healthy church exercises discipline when necessary but never in an irresponsible, reckless, and destructive manner.

(3) "What harmony (*sumphōnēsis*, "agreement") is there between Christ and Belial?"[8] There is no possible harmony or agreement between Christ and Satan. The devil was a murderer and liar from the beginning (John 8:44). Christ is the righteous one who appeared for the purpose of destroying the devil's works (1 John 3:8).

(4) "What does a believer have in common (*meris*, "share") with an unbeliever?" This is not intended to teach that there can be no contact between a believer and unbeliever, but the point is that the Christian faith is exclusive. No one can be a believer and an unbeliever at the same time. There is no in-between. He is either a believer or an unbeliever.

(5) "What agreement is there between the temple (*naos*, "sanctuary," "shrine")[9] of God and idols?" The local church is God's temple. The focus here is on the corporate dwelling.[10] That is, God dwells in the entire Christian community, the Christian fellowship, the Christian society. God's true dwelling

---

[8]Belial (Beliar) refers to Satan, not to the Antichrist.

[9]Temple (*naos*) does not refer to the entire temple area (*hieron*), including the outer courts, porches and other buildings; but it should be understood in the restricted sense of *shrine*. In the Old Testament it was the Holy place or Holy of Holies where the presence of God was manifested.

[10]The best illustration of the Holy Spirit dwelling in the church as a body is stated in 1 Cor. 3:16-17: "Don't you know that you yourselves are God's temple and that God's Spirit lives in you? If anyone destroys God's temple, God will destroy him; for God's temple is sacred, and you are that temple." The church as a body is indwelt by the Holy Spirit, but the church is comprised of individuals—each of whom has become a single temple of God. What is true for the church as a whole is true also for the individuals who are members of the church. See 1 Cor. 6:19.

place is the church, a community of people who have been reconciled to God. Idols should have no place in the Christian community in whose life men and women ought to be able to meet God. This means that the church should not worship modern idols such as money, power, success, and prestige. God and idols are irreconcilable whether they are ancient or modern. Idolatry has no place in the Christian community because of its exclusive relationship with God through Christ. The Church cannot be the temple of God and the temple of Satan at the same time.

2. A biblical basis for separation (6:16b-18).   According to Scripture separation is essential to consecration. Israel had to be brought "out" of Egypt before they could be brought "into" Canaan. Abraham had to "come out" before he could "go in." The series of questions raised by Paul made the same point. That is, there were some things with which Christians could make no compromise and some people with whom they could have no close personal ties. These were serious concerns for Paul, and they should be for us. He underlined the importance of Christians being morally alert and being conscious that there are limits in social relations with unbelievers. He also confirmed this by citing a few examples of what God declared in the Old Testament[11] about the separation of His people from a secular culture:

> I will live with them and walk with them, and I will be their God, and they will be my people.
>
> Therefore come out from them
>   and be separate,
>   says the Lord.
> Touch no unclean thing,
>   and I will receive you.
> I will be a Father to you,
>   and you will be my sons and daughters,
>   says the Lord Almighty (6:16-18).

C. Their Summons to Holiness (7:1)

The presence of God in the church requires the purity of His people. The sons and daughters of God are the people among whom God dwells. As the people

---

[11]See Lev. 26:11f.; Ezek. 37:26f.; Isa. 52:11; Ezek. 20:34.

of God, we are like a temple, the place where God dwells. Are we ashamed of what He sees and hears among us? The fact of God's presence in our midst should have its consequences in holiness of life. Because the lifestyle of believers is so vital to the ministry of reconciliation, the apostle challenged the Corinthians to live a separated life.

1. The basis—the promises of God. Through the divine promises the Corinthians were assured that God would be in their midst. These promises referred back to those about which Paul had already spoken. God had promised them that He would live and walk among them and He would be a father to them (6:16, 18). They had a new identity and a new status as sons and daughters of God. His presence among them was the foundation for Christlike living. As expected of all Christians, the Christian community at Corinth was to live in "blessed communion" with Him and was to reflect in its life that it was a community of reconciliation.

2. The motive—"out of reverence for God." The holy God is the final judge of the community of believers: the ministry and works of Christians will be reviewed by Christ Himself (5:10). This should create in us a sense of deep reverence for God and warn us against any inclination to compromise our faith and against anything that would render us unfit for fellowship with God (see Gal. 5:19-21). God does not dwell with those who persist in sin. The church's accommodation to the values of this fallen world excludes God from its midst. God's people, therefore, are called to be morally alert and to renounce all evil out of reverent respect for God.

3. The aim—striving "for perfection" (hagiōsunēn, *"holiness"*). Holiness is the true response to God's reconciling grace and is a full dedication to what pleases God. The word is associated with health and wholeness and refers to the development and advancement in Christian character. Holiness is the result of a life lived in close fellowship with God.

As indicated by Paul, holiness involves purifying "ourselves from everything that contaminates the body and spirit." This encompasses the whole man—both the body and spirit. The Christian is to be clean in the outer man and allow for no habits, practices, or indulgence that would be defiling and immoral. The Christian must not only guard against the sins of the body but also those of the spirit—animosity, jealousy, hatred, envy, malice, ill-temper, and many others. Evils, whether they are primarily seen as a matter of the outer or inner man, will disrupt our fellowship with God and our relationships with other people. However, holiness is not simply a removal of everything that defiles man; but it is, in fact, the very life of Christ. As those things that contaminate our lives are laid aside, holiness will grow and increase. More and more we are transformed into the likeness of Jesus Christ. Through the Holy Spirit the life of Christ makes our lives holy.

III. CONCLUSION

Every Christian is called to full-time Christian service (*diakonia*) just as surely as the pastor of a church. Thus our thesis is that the ministry of reconciliation is accomplished by the members of the whole Christian community living and serving in every walk of life. As Christians our relationships in and outside of the church are to be good and proper so that the interest of reconciliation is served. This was the stance that Paul took, but for him the work of reconciliation was never easy. It was demanding, and he carried with him a style of life that was a demonstration of reconciling love and holiness. He worked hard to minister to unhealed feelings and to construct good relationships in the church. While he was careful not to become tainted by the corrupting influences in the world, he stood ready to take the gospel to all men and women.

Paul's work in the gospel cost him something. He was misunderstood by the church, and he endured adversities, persecutions, and burdens. At the heart of his Christian experience and ministry was the cross. There is no gospel without the cross, but there are those who seek to empty the gospel of the cross. Many of them are religious profiteers. They preach a faith that is defined as the building of our self-confidence, freeing us from negative thoughts and enabling us to discover the infinite possibilities within ourselves. They declare a gospel that is without a cross to bear and that guarantees us that we will be healthy, wealthy, and wise. They proclaim a faith that assures us of comfort, acceptance, and peace of mind. This cannot be the gospel. Any gospel without the cross is not the gospel of reconciliation. Any gospel without the cross cannot give us strength and hope in the face of troubles and tragedies. Faith in that kind of gospel is like building a house on sand—when the storms of life come, the collapse is certain. A gospel that calls for no sacrifice—a gospel that supposedly assures us of affluent prosperity—a gospel that is romantic and sentimental and disregards the real nature of sin is not the gospel of Jesus and Paul.

The true gospel was what motivated Paul to build good relationships in the church and to be thoroughly Christian in the world. The importance of the purity of the church caused Paul to urge the Corinthian church in its relationship to the world to take a stance that would prevent any compromise of its devotion to God. Therefore, the gospel raises a distinction between the church and the world. At one time some thought the church in certain sectors was too inflexible and stringent in its insistence on its adherence to tradition. For the most part, this is not the problem we are now facing. The problem is trying to accommodate the church and gospel to everything and everyone. God wants His people to stand out as distinct from the world. This is not to be so much in terms of what we "put on" but as the new life flowing out from within to the world in ministry and service.

It is not enough for the church to be holy and moral. The Christian life is not limited to morality. The Christian, indeed the whole church, is expected to be holy, but beyond holiness is mission and ministry. Holiness and mission are distinctive aspects of the Christian life. However, if the church is satisfied simply with holiness, it becomes an introverted institution concerned with its own life but not with the life of the world. But the church's commission is to "go forth" into the world. The church is called to maintain its distinction and its separation from the godless and corrupting elements of a secular culture. Nevertheless, at the same time the church must construct bridges into the world and "go forth" as heralds of the gospel of reconciliation.

7

The Ministry of Mutual Confidence

2 Corinthians 7:2-16

God's people are members of a close-knit fellowship. Scripture uses a number of compound nouns to express this Christian togetherness—"fellow citizens," "fellow heirs," "fellow laborers," "fellow prisoners," "fellow servants," and "fellow soldiers." The Apostles' Creed calls it the "communion of saints." Paul tells us: "You are all sons of God through faith in Christ Jesus" (Gal. 3:26). This spiritual kinship of God's people transcends natural relationships. However, like any family, people of God need each other; they need the warmth, support, strength, and nurture of the Christian fellowship. Openness and trust are so vital to this mutually strengthening fellowship.

The church is more than what meets the eye and is, therefore, more than a visible institution. It is a fellowship which transcends class, race, party, educational levels, and other human divisions. But this does not mean a fellowship of men simply in the sense of human camaraderie or merely in the sense of association with other persons. The church is a holy fellowship, a fellowship "in Christ," "a fellowship in all the burdens and blessings of the Gospel."[1] The church is the fellowship of reconciliation, peace, love, service, and praise.

Needless to say, the fellowship of believers is not insulated from conflict.

---

[1] A.M. Hunter, *Probing the New Testament*, p. 144.

Each church lives in tension. That is as could be expected, for each congregation deals in life-and-death matters in a cosmic struggle of good and evil (Eph. 6:10-17). The church is to resist, with all its strength, the powers and forces of evil in the world; but within every church conflict, dissension, and discord crop up from time to time. Because of this, reconciliation must be an on-going process in the life of the church. Christians must be willing to listen and to forgive. This was a need among the Christians at Corinth. They were offended at Paul. He knew their hurt feelings could become bitterness. Therefore he sought to promote mutual confidence and fellowship and to mend and end the friction.

I. A PLEA FOR AN END TO ESTRANGEMENT (7:2-4)

The apostle had done nothing to diminish the confidence of the Corinthian believers in him. However, there were some who had sought to poison the relations between Paul and the church.[2] This probably began as a whispering campaign.[3] The aim was to make Paul's motives and ministry suspect and to create unloving attitudes toward him. Conscious of that, Paul picked up again his appeal of 6:11-13 for greater affection.

A. Their Reception of Him (7:2-3)

Paul urged the Corinthians to love him as he loved them: "Make room for us in your hearts." He himself had done nothing, as his opponents apparently charged, that would undermine their confidence in him. To assure the Corinthians of this fact, he reminded them of his careful life.

First, he had wronged no one.[4] This was quite general and did not refer to a specific personal injury. Members of the congregation knew that Paul had not

---

[2]It seems to be a reasonable inference that Paul is repudiating accusations that had been made against him. However, some of the older commentators do see this not so much as a response to accusations made by those who sought to slander him but to the malpractices of certain false teachers. Thus according to this interpretation the stress falls on Paul's conduct in contrast to theirs. See Philip E. Hughes, *The Second Epistle to the Corinthians* (New International Commentary on the New Testament), p. 261.

[3]In light of the tone of chapters 10-13 Paul's accusers must have openly attacked his personal integrity and ministry.

[4]In the Greek each of Paul's three denials begin with "no one" (*oudena*) which is followed by a verb in the aorist tense (*ēdikēsamen, ephtheiramen, epleonektēsamen*). This is an emphatic way of stating that he was not guilty of a single act of wrong doing. The three aorists likely point to a particular occasion when he was in Corinth.

treated anyone unjustly. He had been nothing but a good Christian in his dealings with them. All that he had done was in accord with justice, love, and peace.

Second, he had corrupted no one. The charge could have been that he had ruined some people by his doctrine of Christian freedom, that is, what he had taught about freedom from the law was construed to be an invitation to license and loose living. To give Christian freedom an immoral meaning clearly misinterpreted Pauline teaching. Paul wrote: "Shall we go on sinning so that grace may increase? By no means! We died to sin; how can we live in it any longer?" (Rom. 6:1-2). Again: "Do not let sin reign in your mortal body so that you obey its evil desires. Do not offer the parts of your body to sin, as instruments of wickedness, but rather offer yourselves to God, as those who have been brought from death to life; and offer the parts of your body to him as instruments of righteousness" (Rom. 6:12-13). In his letters Paul repeatedly made clear the ethical demands of the gospel. For him Christian freedom was a freedom to please God. Loose living disrupts our friendship with God and is harmful to our relationship with others and to ourselves.

Third, he had exploited no one. Here the word *exploited* (*pleonektō*, "defraud") is a reference to dishonest financial dealings (12:16-18). The charge was untrue. He had not taken money from the Corinthians for his own advantage, for example, by raising an offering for poor Christians in Jerusalem and then lining his own pockets with the money. The apostle was guilty of no such practices and neither should any Christian be guilty of such.

Fourth, he held no grudge against anyone. What the apostle had said was not to condemn the believers at Corinth. He was not accusing them, but clearing himself of malicious charges made by his accusers. His readers had recently become reconciled with him. He had no desire to reopen the old wounds and conflicts. His purpose was to establish the relationship of mutual confidence. So he hastened to assure them of his abiding affection. The bond of love between them was so strong that he would live and die with them. The words *live* and *die* could have referred to the apostle's death and resurrection, which may be seen as strictly personal experiences,[5] but his conviction was that he would everlastingly continue to be united in them in Christian fel-

---

[5] An alternative interpretation is that Paul is not making a theological point but simply expressing his love for the Corinthians. See C.K. Barrett, *The Second Epistle to the Corinthians* (Harper's New Testament Commentaries) p. 204. However, in light of 4:14 the expression "live or die with you" can be understood as a reference to Paul's death and resurrection to be with Christ in the age to come. The fact that in the Greek Paul put *die* before *live* may be understood to support this interpretation. The redeemed are united in an everlasting fellowship.

lowship and love. Paul loved them so deeply. They were not just in his heart but in his heart to live or die together. So far as he was concerned, nothing would separate them; they were one in life and death.

A change of circumstances does not impair true love, not even death can destroy it (1 Cor. 13:13). In such love is no room for the bearing of a grudge and for entertaining bitterness. Love ought always to bind together those who are brothers and sisters in Christ. It is a solid and everlasting basis for mutual confidence and fellowship.

B. His Confidence in Them (7:4)

The Corinthians were not always model Christians, but the good report brought by Titus had filled Paul with confidence in them.[6] As one who had devoted his whole life to the ministry of reconciliation, the apostle took the greatest satisfaction in knowing that the breach between himself and the Corinthian believers had been healed. Mutual confidence had been reestablished. He wanted to remove any doubt that they might have had about his confidence in them.

First, Paul had great pride in them. A literal rendering here of what he said is: "I can boast freely about you." That is, when he spoke about them to others, he spoke now proudly of their faith and loyalty. Indeed he did just that to Titus: "I had boasted to him about you, and you have not embarrassed me. But just as everything we said to you was true, so our boasting about you to Titus has proved to be true as well" (7:14). Too, he has spoken freely about the Corinthians' willingness to contribute to the fund for poverty-stricken saints in Jerusalem: "For I know your eagerness to help, and I have been boasting about it to the Macedonians, telling them that since last year you in Achaia were ready to give; and your enthusiasm has stirred most of them to action" (9:2). Sincere commendations are very much in order and do strengthen human relationships.

Second, Paul was greatly encouraged toward them. The church at Corinth had had troubles, but its rebellion had ended. Due to the news brought by Titus, he was encouraged. The literal meaning of Paul's words here is: "I abound in joy beyond measure." He went on to say: "In all our troubles my joy knows no bounds." The confidence, courage, and joy which he experienced

---

[6]Paul had anxiously waited for Titus at Troas. He discontinued the narrative at 2:13, but at 7:5 he took it up again. This has led to the view that 2:14—7:4 is a digression; and, too, it reminds us that 2 Corinthians is a spontaneous letter.

were experienced in all of his afflictions and hardships. Not just after troubles were over and suffering had ended, but in the midst of them he was filled with confidence, courage, and joy. Throughout his life he carried around in his body the death of Christ (4:10), but his joy and comfort far exceeded any tribulation he endured. His joy overflowed on the occasion that he heard the Corinthians were reconciled to him.

It becomes clear that the apostle strove not only to reconcile men to God but also to himself. He regained the confidence of the Corinthian church. Today there are churches in which pastor and congregation need to be reconciled. In some churches alienation grows out of ministerial and worship styles. Church members may like a certain style of pulpit ministry and will not accept a pastor who is different regardless of how devout and effective he is. A pastor may view a church's worship as dead simply because its style is different from his own. He may prefer gospel songs and choruses; they may demand the traditional hymns or they may like a more sedate worship. He may appreciate enthusiastic handclapping. These differences do give rise to church frictions and disagreements and to human alienations. If discord and conflict are handled in love and wisdom, they can be resolved. Every believer must realize that he shares the responsibility for keeping peace in the family of God and for promoting mutual confidence among the members of the household of faith.

II. A MESSAGE OF COMFORT (7:5-7)

In 2:12-13 the apostle began to tell about the occasion when Titus failed to meet him in Troas. After a short stay in the city, he pressed on into Macedonia where Titus came to him with good news about the spiritual well-being of the Corinthian believers. However, at 2:14 Paul turned aside to thank God for blessing his ministry and then went on to discuss at some length the ministry of reconciliation. Only at 7:5 did he proceed to describe his wait for Titus in Macedonia. Paul was thinking of resuming the account in verse 4, where he reflected the new confidence, encouragement, and joy that the good news brought. Before receiving the welcomed news he had great anxiety about whether the Corinthians had accepted Titus and his ministry and what their response had been to the chastening letter. The apostle described himself before and after he met Titus in Macedonia.

A. His Feeling of Strain (7:5)

Before Titus arrived the situation at Macedonia was dreadful for Paul. It was no better for him than it had been in Troas. He was full of restless tensions and distress. "This body of ours," he said, "had no rest, but we were harassed at every turn—conflicts on the outside, fears within." He had bitter conflicts from without. His adversaries, either Macedonian Christians or unbelievers, attacked him. They filled the air with strife and animosity. To compound the troubles he had inward fears also. He had no idea how the Corinthians had received his letter, but he had fear of receiving a bad report. Too, Titus was seriously overdue. The apostle must have wondered if he had fallen into peril and was concerned about the young man's safety. Fears gnawed at Paul's heart. He was outwardly persecuted and inwardly perplexed.

Conflicts and fears are common to the experience of any believer. We all have had conflicts of one kind or another. We have had fears of one kind or another. Of one thing we may be certain, Paul was not defeated by his troubles. The truth is, his conflicts and fears made him a better servant of Jesus Christ. God has a way of making adversities, whether outward or inward, serve the ministry of reconciliation. An awareness of this should give us a positive attitude toward suffering for Jesus' sake.

B. Titus, God's Messenger of Comfort (7:6-7)

God brought comfort to His servant Paul, who was in great need of encouragement. The letter that had been sent to Corinth by Paul was a rebuke of sin and required sinners to be disciplined.[7] He had distressful anxiety about the state of affairs at Corinth. When Titus arrived in Macedonia, his burden was lifted and his fears were swept away. There was nothing like divine consolation. Out of gratitude the apostle described God as the one "who comforts the downcast." Through the good news from Corinth God drove away the apostle's anxious misgivings and filled his heart with comfort and joy. The success of Paul's reconciling work was obvious. Now there was harmony and confidence between the Corinthians and himself. So he went on to explain why he was comforted by the good news from their city.

1. He was comforted by the Corinthians' reception of Titus (7:7a). Reunion with Titus, his friend and co-laborer, gave him joy. Indeed, he was more than pleased that the young man had been restored to him safe and sound. However, revival among the Corinthians did not only gladden Paul; Titus rejoiced that "the walls of rejection" had fallen down. It was possible that Titus had undertaken his mission to Corinth with misgivings and had arrived in the

---

[7]See 2:4; 7:8.

city in low spirits. He did not encounter what he might have expected—antagonism, disputes, church fights. On the contrary, the Corinthians were obedient. Their change of attitude toward Paul brought comfort to Titus. When he met the apostle later, "he did not only bring comfort, but he brought it out of a heart that had drunk in all the comfort in Corinth."[8]

2. The apostle was comforted by the welcome changes at Corinth (7:7).   The reconciliation of the Corinthians was marked by three significant changes. First, they longed to see Paul. They earnestly desired to see the apostle in person. Earlier he had planned to visit them, but he decided it would be better to stay away rather than pay them another painful visit (2:1). He had sent Titus. They now yearned to see him and to restore cordial relations and confidence between themselves and him. Now their hearts were open to him.

Second, the Corinthians were repentant for what they had done. They had caused him so much trouble and grief. In order to spare the Corinthians he had postponed a visit to them (1:23). He did not want, for their sakes, a repeat of the unhappy experience of his second visit. Their behavior had called forth Paul's reproof. They had had a change of heart. The pain they had caused the apostle they deeply regretted.

Third, they had an ardent concern for Paul. Their lukewarmness and antagonism had been replaced with enthusiasm, zeal, and devotion. They had become eager to satisfy their apostle. They now stood firmly with him. Before the healing of the rift, affection, sorrow, and concern had been all on his side. But now, to his joy, that had been changed. The thrice-repeated *your* spoke volumes—"*your* affection, *your* deep sorrow, *your* ardent concern."

The apostle's worries and troubles had been great, but he was willing to forget the unhappy past. It is no surprise that God used him mightily in the ministry of reconciliation. The apostle loved dearly his converts at Corinth. Their restored devotion to the apostle rested on the gospel in which he labored. They were faithful to him because they recognized him to be a true servant of Christ. Woe to those who attach people to themselves rather than to Jesus Christ.

III. A RESTORATION OF MUTUAL CONFIDENCE
(7:8-12)

Why had Paul felt such great joy? Was it because of the Corinthians' humiliation—the pain that he had caused them? His rejoicing could have seemed un-

---

[8]R.C.H. Lenski, *Interpretation of I and II Corinthians*, p. 1103.

kind. He was, therefore, careful to show why he had such joy and to remove any possibility of misunderstanding.

A. His Concern About the Stern Letter (7:8-9a)

The painful letter Paul had written grieved the Corinthians. After he sent it, the apostle had some misgivings, even regret about the letter. He did not know what effect it would have. There was no way of knowing what the response of the Corinthians might be—whether they would repent or whether their relationship with Paul would become more strained. No doubt, he was anxious about the outcome. But when he heard of the result—that they had completely changed their attitude—he was so glad that he had written the letter. His exultant joy was proper and justified. As he said, "I see that my letter hurt you, but only for a little while—yet now I am happy, not because you were made sorry, but because your sorrow led you to repentance."

B. His Concern About the Nature of Their Sorrow (7:9b-11)

The heart of Paul had been gladdened because his letter had led the Corinthian believers to genuine repentance. His letter could have made them angry or despondent and could have produced only superficial regret that their relationship had been strained. In no way would that have awakened a real conviction of sin. The letter, however, did produce grief for their sin against God. The Corinthians became sorrowful "as God intended." They were truly repentant. This led the apostle to analyze the two kinds of sorrow.

First, "Godly sorrow brings repentance." It is the way to reconciliation, to harmony with God and man. It "leads to salvation and leaves no regret." Never will those who have experienced godly sorrow regret it. On them is bestowed the divine gift of salvation. Sin causes alienation and misery, but God's reconciling grace motivated the Corinthians to harbor no longer any resentment against Paul and to seek renewal of fellowship. Grievances were wiped out. Mutual confidence was restored. There was an abandonment of sin. Lives were changed. The church was strengthened. Love and peace prevailed in the Christian fellowship.

Those who truly repent do not suffer loss. But godly remorse always leads to the very opposite—the greatest spiritual gain. The repentant Corinthians would never need to feel any regret. Godly sorrow led them to a renewal of their fellowship with God and Paul. God had forgiven them as He has us. It is well for us to remember Paul's words when he wrote: "Be kind and compassionate to one another, forgiving each other, just as in Christ God forgave you" (Eph. 4:32).

Second, "worldy sorrow brings death." There is a difference between worldly remorse and true repentance. Worldly sorrow is fatal; it leads to death. It is the consequence of sin and may be awakened by the loss of friends, health, possessions, power, and self-respect. When people experience worldly sorrow, there is pain; but in their remorse is no sense of wrong done. They dislike the pain, but it does not drive them to seek God's forgiveness. They do not deal with their real trouble at all. The disease, which only true repentance will cure, is not treated but just the symptoms. In the case of a broken relationship, peace may be sought by a half-hearted apology or by offering some excuse such as "I'm not perfect." No real effort, however, is put forth toward fundamental reconciliation. Only the symptoms of the disease are dealt with but not the real disease that lies at the root of alienation. The healing of a broken relationship requires godly sorrow which produces a conviction of sin and a spirit of honesty and humility.

Worldly sorrow leads nowhere but to spiritual death. The man who hates his sin not because it is a wrong against God but because of the pain it causes him has not experienced godly sorrow that works repentance. The Corinthians did not feel this fatal worldly grief, but theirs was the kind that was wrought and approved by God. The changes in the life and character of the Corinthians were marks of true repentance. The apostle used seven words to describe what Godly sorrow had induced in them.

(1) Earnestness. The Christians at Corinth had dropped their indifference. They had taken prompt and decisive action to deal with the spiritual and moral conditions in the church. No longer did they see these as small matters. In all earnestness they were busy putting things in moral and spiritual order.

(2) Eagerness. This was obvious in their desire to clear themselves. Godly grief led them to give an account of their earlier indifference and inactivity. Perhaps scandal had been in the church, and they were now eager to make it clear that they had not been involved. They did not want it thought that they had been accomplices in wrong doing. They were determined to prove their innocence.

(3) Indignation. Presumably this was their reaction either to the scandal that they might have permitted in the church or to a troublemaker in the church (2:5). Now they took a stand and were indignant at sin.

(4) Alarm (*phobos*, "fear"). They were more fully awake and aware of the real spiritual dangers of sin and especially of its disruptive impact on their fellowship. More than ever they were sensitive to the will of God.

(5) Affection (*epipothēsis*, "longing"). The longing was for Paul himself. He was the apostle of the Corinthian Christians. Their desire was to be reunited with him who had preached to them reconciliation and to restore their fellowship of mutual trust and affection.

(6) Concern (*zēlos*, "zeal"). They were zealously devoted to Paul and to the service of Jesus Christ.

(7) Justice (*ekdikesis*, "punishment"). They were ready to see justice done and to inflict punishment on anyone who disrupted the fellowship of the church.

These were signs of genuine repentance and reconciliation. Now that the Corinthians were spiritually renewed Paul did not want to dwell on the past. He preferred to commend the church for taking decisive action to punish his opposition. The repentance of the Corinthians was not due to any wrong they had done but to their failure at first to discipline one who had done wrong (2:5). Negligence in dealing with flagrant sin in the church has a disrupting effect on Christian fellowship.

C. His Concern About Their Loyalty (7:12)

When Paul wrote the "severe letter" he was not so much concerned either with the person who did wrong[9] or the one who had suffered injury. His foremost concern was their loyalty to him and to the gospel which he preached. So his motive for writing to the Corinthians was not to seek revenge, but as Hughes has expressed it so well:

> ... he hoped by this letter to bring home to them a clear realization of their true relationship to him, as being in reality bound to him by the deepest bonds of affection and loyalty. To a greater or lesser degree the trouble-makers in Corinth had succeeded in casting a cloud over this relationship; but none the less he was the spiritual father of that church and he trusted that his letter would remind its members of that fact and fan the spark of devotion which, he was sure, still glowed within their hearts. Thus the cloud of disloyalty and disrespect would be removed and the true and proper emotions of their hearts would be revealed to them—not, however, before Paul, as though his concern was for the repair of his wounded dignity rather than for the glory of God, but in the sight of God, for it was nothing less than their spiritual integrity which was at stake.[10]

---

[9]Probably "the one who did the wrong" was the offender whom the church had punished according to 2:5-11 and "the injured party" was Paul himself or perhaps one of his co-workers such as Timothy. Likely Paul's leadership was challenged by the offender who was a ringleader of a revolt and the church did not at that time come to the apostle's defense.

[10]Philip E. Hughes, *The Second Epistle to the Corinthians* (New International Commentary on the New Testament) p. 276.

All that was in the past. The Corinthians had laid aside their resentment and bitterness and were obedient to the gospel and were loyal supporters of Paul. However, he did not hesitate to speak of his past painful relationship with them; it was not that he wished to open an old sore. But as one who understood human relations, he knew that a sure sign of complete restoration of mutual confidence was when the parties involved were able to talk about their past hurts and estrangements. The healing of a relationship is complete only when the parties can talk about their conflicts without placing a strain on the new relationship. When this can be done, the hurts have been emptied of all their bitterness; and the healing of the relationship is complete. The result is that those who have been at odds are drawn together into a deeper commitment and a closer fellowship. Friction wisely resolved in the church means moving ahead for God's glory. Truly happy are those whose relations have been stormy, but now there is peace and mutual confidence.

IV. AN OVERFLOW OF JOY AND COMFORT (7:13-16)

The changes of the hearts of his spiritual children gave Paul good reason to be encouraged. But he had another reason for rejoicing still more. The joy of Titus confirmed Paul's confidence in the Corinthians; and it, too, added to the intensity of his joy.

A. The Rejoicing and Affection of Titus (7:13, 15)

Titus must have been aware of the faults of the Corinthians. Paul had assured him that fundamentally they were sound. What they had done even to Paul did not make the apostle blind to their better qualities. On the whole he had confidence in them. Doubtless before arriving in Corinth Titus was deeply concerned about the belligerent attitude of the Corinthians. He was aware of the schisms in the church and must have had misgivings about how he would be received by the Corinthians. His reception was not anything like he had expected. His visit of Corinth turned out to be a delightful experience. Learning of their response to his colleague greatly increased Paul's own joy. "We were especially delighted," Paul wrote the Corinthians, "to see how happy Titus was, because all of you helped to put his mind at ease."

The Corinthians had received Titus with great respect and listened intently to the "stern letter." They reacted to his message "with fear and trembling."

This reminds us that Paul began his work at Corinth "in weakness and fear, and with much trembling" (1 Cor. 2:3). Apparently before Titus arrived they had already begun to realize their Christian responsibility and had returned their loyalty to Paul. By the time Titus entered the city the walls of alienation had fallen down and reconciling grace had healed the rift. They were ready to obey the word of God. Because of appreciation and love on both sides the spirit of mutual confidence was restored between the church and Paul.

Titus did not forget what happened. He had in his heart a more intense affection for the Corinthians than before.

B. The Boast of Paul (7:14)

Titus was sent to Corinth with the "severe letter." Prior to his departure Paul had boasted of the Corinthians to him, but his praise was restrained (*ti*, "somewhat"). There was not much he could be proud of at the time. Even so, he did not lose sight of the good traits of the congregation. His confidence and praise might have appeared to be more than warranted, but the apostle was happy to report that his praise of them to Titus had been verified: "I had boasted to him about you, and you have not embarrassed me."

Some good things were said by Paul about the Corinthian church. He knew that dwelling on their faults and talking behind their backs would do nothing but deepen the resentment and bitterness and increase estrangement. This is a truth of which we all need to be aware. When we depreciate others and are harsh in our criticism of them, it is an attempt at self-vindication more than anything else. Everyone has some good qualities. Paul spoke the truth in his "severe letter" in which he rebuked the Corinthians for their failing, but what he said in commendation of them was true also. The test of what is said is truth, but even truth needs to be tempered with love. It is love that turns friction and misunderstanding into cementing fellowship. As Jesus said, "All men will know that you are my disciples if you love one another" (John 13:35).

C. The Joy of Confidence (7:16)

Paul had had some agony over the Corinthians and had invested concern and prayer in them. Now he was happy. The dark clouds had passed and an unpleasant situation had ended well. His efforts had begun to pay dividends of love, joy, and peace within that Christian fellowship.

All the misgivings had disappeared. Paul had come to the happy state of perfect confidence in the congregation. He concluded with these words: "I am glad I can have complete confidence in you."[11]

V. CONCLUSION

Among some Christians there is a dearth of confidence. A lack of confidence in one another splits us apart and cuts us off from one another. At one time the Corinthians did not have confidence in Paul and were estranged from the apostle who had brought to them the gospel. His effort and concern were to restore their confidence. He knew that if they did not trust him they would have little confidence in his message. Their reconciliation with God and with him was rooted in Christ. These two dimensions of reconciliation were to be simultaneous with each other, but there were factors which drove a wedge between Paul and his friends at Corinth.

Today the church, the community of reconciliation, is no stranger to factors that create tension and disrupt its fellowship. Among these are: honest misunderstanding—that grows out of inadequate communication; difference of opinion—one may have a closed mind and see any difference of judgment as a breach of fellowship; difference of approach—this may create tension and misunderstanding; difference of experience—past experience of two friends can run counter to each other and lead to the breaking of personal relationship; too much contact—the truth is that familiarity does breed contempt; too little contact—good human relations thrive on communication and fellowship; keen competition—few people can maintain good human relations when they are zealously competing for the same possession, whether it is for the attention of another person or for personal prestige and power; pride and selfishness—these are closely aligned and will endanger any friendship; lack of candor—alienation develops when friends are unable to be candid with one another;[12] the old ways and new ways of doing things—conflict often rises be-

---

[11]Reconciliation reported here need not be understood to be a total one and consequently incompatible with Paul's large-scale defense of his ministry in chapters 10-13. Apparently there was still some tension in the church which was created by fake apostles who had invaded the church. When Paul refers to the Corinthian repentance and innocence, he qualifies the experience "At every point" with the specific "in this matter" (7:11). There were still some lingering problems since he was defensive about his travel plans (1:15ff.), his letters (1:12; 2:3ff.) and his general trustworthiness (1:12, 18-22).

[12]I am indebted for these insights to J. Martin Bailey, *From Wrecks to Reconciliation*, pp. 35-38.

tween the traditionalists and innovators; young and old people—people of different ages frequently have different goals.

Indeed, when these factors drive wedges between Christians, carnality is at the root of it even though they may in measure be due to the natural distinctions such as age, sex, race, etc. The church is a community of reconciliation which embraces likes and unlikes. One may choose his friends but not his brothers and sisters. Friendship may be ended, but brothers remain brothers, even in conflict. Communion of saints is a brotherhood that is to be characterized by mutual trust and by mutual love. To ensure that it is just that, every Christian is to be a minister of reconciliation and thus should put forth a consistent effort to promote mutual confidence and love in the body of Christ.

8

The Ministry of Christian Giving

2 Corinthians 8:1-24

The renewed loyalty of the Corinthians had justified Paul's confidence in them. After mutual confidence had been restored, Paul went on to introduce the subject of giving and to speak of the relief fund which he was organizing among the missionary churches for the needy Christians in Jerusalem. This fund, known also as the collection (*logeia*), is referred to in Romans 15:25-32, 1 Cor. 16:1-4, Gal. 2:10, and Acts 24:17. The collection for the church at Jerusalem was dear to the heart of Paul. Chapters 8 and 9 of 2 Corinthians were his reminder to the Corinthians to give a generous sum of money to the fund (9:11, 13). It was a way they could minister to the needs of the poor Christians in the Jerusalem church.

Giving is fundamental to the Christian ministry.[1] "Two main instruments for the fulfillment of the ministry ... are money on the one side and actual work on the other."[2] Money is no substitute for personal involvement in the ministry of reconciliation. But just as the women of Luke 8:2-3 ministered to Jesus and the twelve apostles "out of their own means" so Christians today should

---

[1]Noteworthy is the fact that Paul used *diakonia* ("service, ministry") as a fundamental designation of his ministry (Rom. 11:12; 1 Cor. 3:5; 2 Cor. 3:6; 4:1; 5:18), but also he employed various forms of the same word in reference to the collection project (Rom. 15:25; 2 Cor. 8:4, 19; 9:1, 12, 13).

[2]G.W. Bromiley, *Christian Ministry.* p. 69.

minister by giving generously and sacrificially. Obviously gifts of money cannot give spiritual power to the message of reconciliation, but the church has a responsibility to minister to those who face hunger and want. Furthermore, equipment, buildings, and their maintenance are almost indispensable to the ministry. The provision of these practical needs and aids demands sacrificial giving of the church and is a form of ministry. G.W. Bromiley reminds us:

> The giving of money is not, therefore, merely an act of stewardship as usually represented. It is this. But it is also an act of ministry in the deepest sense, and it is to be performed as such, not with a reliance upon money or pride in its material power, but in the power of the Holy Spirit and the obedience, faith and love of genuine discipleship.[3]

The ministry of giving occupied a significant place in the life of the early church. Paul urged the Corinthians to assume their responsibility in this ministry by contributing to the fund that he was raising for the church in Jerusalem. Before we consider the appeal Paul made to the Corinthians, it may be well to place the collection project in perspective.

I. THE FUND FOR THE NEEDY CHRISTIANS IN JERUSALEM

Obviously the apostle was keenly interested in the success of this project. He must have devoted a great deal of time to its promotion.

A. Its Model

The aid sent by the young church at Antioch to Jerusalem provided the pattern for the Pauline collection among the Gentile churches. The Christians in Antioch learned of the state of affairs in the Holy City from those who fled Jerusalem to escape persecution (Acts 11:19) and from Barnabas (Acts 11:22). Agabus also had appeared in Antioch and told of a famine that would soon fall on Jerusalem (Acts 11:27-28). The church there received his prophecy and prepared to raise funds for their Jerusalem brethren. Apparently the situation did become more critical than it had been and the Antioch Christians sent the money that they had gathered by Paul and Barnabas (Acts 11:30). This action

---

[3]*Ibid.*, p. 70.

of the Christian community at Antioch was the model for the collection raised by Paul for the mother church in Jerusalem.[4]

B. Its Significance

There were at least two motives for Paul's interest in the success of the relief fund.

1. An act of Christian charity.   Many of the members of the Christian community at Jerusalem were poor (Acts 6:1ff.). The community's financial position became worse. Crowds of pilgrims came to the Holy City at the times of the great feasts. On these occasions demands for charity and hospitality were great. Food was scarce because the demand was greater than the supply, but it was only Christian for the Jerusalem church to minister to the needs of both the Jews and Jewish Christians. The bitter persecutions which befell the Christians in the city must have swept away the homes of Christians and their means of employment (Acts 4:1ff.; 5:17ff.; 6:12ff.; 7:54ff.; 15:1f.). They were hard pressed and in desperate need. Therefore the collection which Paul raised among his missionary churches was an act of Christian charity. Among the early Christians charity was vital to Christian fellowship. It was one expression of fellowship in Christ and a ministry of love.

2. An instrument of reconciliation.   The collection was a simple expression of Christian charity, but for Paul it was that and more too. Through the missionary outreach of Paul and others there was an influx of Gentiles into the church. As a result tension developed in the body of Christ between Jew and Gentile. At times this led to the disruption of the unity in a few of the local churches.[5] The collection helped Paul to bind Jewish and Gentile Christians together in a bond of brotherhood. The Gentiles, the newcomers to the faith, gave contributions to the veterans, the Jewish Christians of the mother church. Thus the collection was more than a means of relieving distress. Its

---

[4]See Keith F. Nickle, *The Collection*, pp. 24-29.

[5]Tension between Jewish and Gentile Christians emerges here and there in the New Testament, but especially it is seen in the proceedings at the Jerusalem Council (Acts 15) and in the conflict between Paul and Peter at Antioch (Gal. 2:11-21). The problem was so acute that the church at Antioch sent Paul and Barnabas to confer with apostles and elders at Jerusalem about the matter (Acts 15:2). To promote reconciliation among Jewish and Gentile believers the "Apostolic Decrees" were sent as a guide for the preservation of unity in the church (Acts 15:22-29).

aim, too, was to express and preserve Christian unity.[6] Complete reconciliation of Jew and Gentile is reflected in Ephesians 2:16, where we are told that Christ has "reconcile[d] both of them to God through the cross, by which he put to death their hostility." The collection, therefore, was a means used by Paul to promote concord in the church communities, cementing Jew and Gentile together and bringing to realization in Christian fellowship what Christ accomplished through the cross.

II. THE PRACTICE OF GIVING (8:1-15)

Beginning his appeal, Paul called to mind a great example of Christian generosity and of work to break down racial barriers disrupting the unity of the church. The example was the sacrifices of the Macedonian Christians.[7] The apostle challenged the Corinthians to emulate this example.

A. The Example of the Macedonian Believers (8:1-15)

Speaking of their giving, Paul emphasized five things.

1. *It was evidence of the grace* (charis, *"generosity," "gift") of God (8:1).* Through the ministry of the apostle, God had freely bestowed on the Macedonians His reconciling grace. Divine grace gave them a new orientation and gave them concern for Christian fellowship and for the Jewish Christians. Concern was inspired by God's grace. What God did for the Macedonian Christians prompted their generosity. Their contributions to the collection were evidence of the grace of God at work.

2. *It was in the midst of severe trial and extreme poverty (8:2).* The Macedonian churches had endured great difficulties. On the whole Macedonia was prosperous, but the hand of Roman occupation pressed hard upon the country. The Imperial Crown had seized the affluent silver and gold mines and had taxed heavily the importation of salt and the smelting of copper. The prof-

---

[6]I am indebted for these insights to Keith F. Nickle, *The Collection*, pp. 100-143. Dr. Nickle not only understands Paul's collection to have been an expression of Christian charity and an action aimed at cementing Jews and Christians together but also to be an anticipation of Christian eschatology.

[7]The churches of Macedonia were at Thessalonica, Philippi, and Berea.

[8]C.K. Barrett, *The Second Epistle to the Corinthians* (Harper's New Testament Commentaries), p. 219.

itable timber industry for shipbuilding was likewise controlled.[8] The Christians, moreover, had suffered severe afflictions for their faith (Phil. 1:29-30; 1 Thess. 1:6; 2:14; 3:3-5; 2 Thess. 1:4-10). To a great extent their poverty was the result of persecution. Far from frustrating the Christian spirit, these hardships of oppression and poverty made it more ardent. There was "overflowing joy" in the midst of great afflictions and there was "rich generosity" in the midst of poverty. God was at work in the hearts of the Macedonian Christians. Their joy in God's fellowship had released them from the love of money and had given them a concern about the needs of others.

The spirit of generosity is a mark of fellowship with God. Christians who have little and have to struggle to make ends meet often surprise us with their joy, love, and victory. They have real wealth. They have hidden treasure. They have deep fellowship with God. That makes them more than just religious. It makes them true disciples of Christ and victorious Christians, even in the midst of hardship and sacrifice.

3. It was liberal (8:3). The Christians in Macedonia "gave as much as they were able and even beyond their ability." They had not given out of abundance but out of "extreme poverty"[9] (v. 2). Their poverty was not going continually deeper and deeper; rather it had already reached rock bottom. It was a "down to earth" poverty. Their gifts could not have been enormous. Consequently what Paul had in mind was not the amount they gave but their attitude. They gave "even beyond their ability"—not according to their means but beyond it.

The will and motive of the giver are so important. The liberal giver is not necessarily the one who gives large sums but the one who gives in proportion to his ability. Men are prone to estimate liberality by the size of the gift, but God measures it by the size of the balance. One day in Jerusalem Jesus observed rich people who gave large amounts to the temple treasury, but a poor widow put in only two small copper coins, worth about a penny. Jesus said to His disciples: "I tell you the truth, this poor widow has put more into the treasury than all the others. They all gave out of their wealth; but she, out of her poverty, put in everything—all she had to live on" (Mark 12:43-44).

4. It was voluntary (8:4). The Macedonians participated spontaneously in the ministry of giving. There was no pressure, for they gave "entirely on their

---

[9]Their poverty was a profound reality. The Greek (*kata bathous*) literally means "down-to-the-depths."

own." Though they themselves were poor, they were prepared to do their part for the poor saints in Jerusalem. They gave on their own accord more than what they could comfortably afford.

Besides, we notice, the Macedonian Christians insisted on giving. For them giving was not a duty but a privilege. They entreated Paul to allow them the privilege to share in the "fellowship of the ministry"[10] to the poor Christians in Jerusalem. Giving was one way they participated in the ministry of reconciliation. No Christian should pass up the opportunity to do the same.

5. It was a witness of commitment to Christ (8:5).   A specific characteristic of the liberality of the Macedonian Christians was that they surrendered all to Christ. They gave their money, but the essential point is "they gave themselves first to the Lord." Their offering themselves entirely to Christ was of first importance, but then they pledged their loyalty to Paul "in keeping with the will of God." Their complete devotion and self-surrender made the giving of their means easy. They placed themselves completely at Paul's disposal for the service of Christ. The result of their self-surrender was more than mere liberality with their money. It led to the giving of themselves to their apostle, a trusted servant of Christ. It is possible for us to give our money without giving ourselves. However, to give ourselves along with our gifts reveals God's reconciling grace in action.

At the root of genuine liberality is the consecration of our whole life to the service of Christ and to others. What we have really belongs to the Lord. He has entrusted to us material goods and gifts. As His stewards we all are accountable for the way we use them (Matt. 25:14-30).

B. An Exhortation to the Corinthian Believers (8:6-8; 10-15)

The example of the Macedonians had been put before them. The Corinthians were better off than the Macedonians. Not only were they, therefore, capable of imitating but also of surpassing the Macedonians. The citing of the example of the Macedonians in giving was to prompt the Corinthians to the same action. The apostle called to the attention of the believers at Corinth four particulars about the collection.

1. It should be brought to completion (8:6, 10-12).   Paul had been encouraged by the generosity of the Macedonians. So he had urged Titus to return to Corinth

---

[10]The New International Version renders the phrase (*ten koinōnian tes diakonias*) as "sharing in the service."

and to complete "this act of grace," that is, the collection. This gracious work had been begun by Titus some time ago[11] but had been checked by dissensions which had broken out earlier among the Corinthian Christians. As we have already seen, that had been cleared up. Now it was time to get on with the good work without any further delay.

Paul's urging of them to complete the collection was both bold and tactful. He did not issue any commands, but he made note first, of their liberality—"you were the first not only to give but also to have the desire to do so" and second, of their readiness—"that your eager willingness to do it may be matched by your completion of it." The work could be finished if now they were ready to give. Once they decided to renew what they had begun a year ago, the job would be completed. The fact was that God would accept their gift on the basis of what they had, not on what they did not have.

The Corinthians were not counseled by Paul to give beyond their means nor to sell all they had and give to the poor of Jerusalem.[12] They knew that they ought to give something. Paul wanted them to get on with it. Their gift would be acceptable however small it might be. The important thing was for them to do what they could. God never asks for what we do not have. Nor does He expect us to give above and beyond our ability.

2. It was in the "grace of giving" that they should excel (8:7). The Corinthians were a tremendously gifted church and blessed with Christian virtues. "You excel," Paul reminded them, "in everything—in faith, in speech, in knowledge, in complete earnestness and in your love for us." But he went on to urge them to measure up to their capabilities. If they did, they would "also excel in this grace of giving." They had been outstanding in every way—in faith, in speech, in knowledge, in earnestness, and in love for Paul—except in gracious giving. This grace of giving also was a gift. Therefore the Corinthians were exhorted by Paul to excel, too, in this kind of ministry. They were perfectly capable of surpassing even the Macedonians!

The Christian fellowship at Corinth had an abundance of the charismatic gifts and virtues but to them they needed to add the grace of giving. Through giving there is an outflow of the inflow of God's blessings. Devotion that does

---

[11]Titus probably began the collection when he carried 1 Corinthians, if he was the bearer of this letter, or when he took the "severe letter."

[12]Paul did not urge the Christians to leave everything and live a life of poverty. He neither condemned wealth nor glorified its renunciation. The concern of Paul was that the Christian community provide alms for the needy, but it was never pressed by him to undermine self-respect and self-reliance (1 Thess. 4:12).

not include interest in others becomes a stagnant pool. Behind giving in love is divine grace. A real appreciation of God's generosity should motivate us to minister to the needy.

3. It should be done willingly (8:8). Christian love could not be a product of compulsion. Paul's desire was not to compel the Corinthians to give. He had no intention of issuing commands; but he did admit that his purpose was to use the Macedonians, who had been remarkably generous in the face of extreme poverty, as an incentive to goad them. He wished to test their Christian spirit by comparing it with the Christians of Macedonia. Their zeal should have been at least equal, if it did not surpass, that of the Macedonian churches.

Not at any time had the apostle lorded over the Corinthians (1:24). He wanted their money for the poverty-stricken Christians in Jerusalem. More than just money, he also sought to test the sincerity of their love and to develop Christian character through the ministry of giving. The Corinthians had to make the decision for themselves. God does not force this ministry on anyone, though He may sharply spur us to be liberal givers. The test of faithfulness in giving is not in the amount of our gift but our willingness to give what we can. "The gift is acceptable according to what one has, not according to what he does not have" (v. 12).

4. It should be according to the rule of equality (8:13-15). There was again a change in the appeal. The apostle has urged the Corinthians to complete the collection, to excel in this grace and to do it willingly, but he passed on to the related theme of equality.

Some of the Corinthians had probably objected to the Jerusalem relief fund. The motive for this fund was not to work a hardship on them. There was no thought that the Corinthians and Jerusalem saints should change places—poverty in Corinth and affluence in Jerusalem. The appeal was for the Corinthians to assume their fair share of the responsibility for the project. The method Paul endorsed was that those who had more than they needed share what they had with those in want. Their giving was to be on the basis of equality.[13] This equality was a mutual give and take, a reciprocity, between the Corinthians and the Christians in Jerusalem. The believers at Corinth were to

---

[13]The apostle did not minimize the importance of sacrificial giving: "Whoever sows sparingly will also reap sparingly, and whoever sows generously will also reap generously" (9:6). He did suggest that there should be a sharing with those in need, but this was not a sort of equality that would destroy property ownership nor that would recommend that anyone should surrender his possessions to a communal fund.

give financial help to Jerusalem Christians to meet their present need; but sometime in the future circumstances might be reversed. Should that happen then the Jerusalem church would share with their Gentile brothers in Corinth; consequently there would be equality.

To illustrate his point, Paul cited the case of the Israelites who gathered manna in the wilderness: "He that gathered much did not have too much, and he that gathered little did not have too little" (Exod. 16:18). There was an abundance of manna, but each was to gather only what he needed. The Israelites overcome by greed gathered together all their pots and pans and filled them with manna. It was far more than what they could use, and it would not keep. By the next morning the manna had become foul and offensive. Equality was God's method in regard to the manna. The end was that all had what they needed. Selfishness was not the best policy—an added incentive for the Corinthians to be generous with their gifts to the Jerusalem church. The Israelites who hoarded manna found that the surplus was unusable. Their greed did not pay.

We, too, can be guilty of the same as we gather the good things of life. To avoid this mistake, let us use the surplus for the good of those in want and for the glory of God. To hold tenaciously to the goods of this life, whether we have much or little, is to deny ourselves the privilege of sharing in the ministry of giving.

C. The Supreme Example of Generosity (8:9)

Having appealed to the enthusiastic, spontaneous, sincere response of the Macedonians, Paul now appealed to the supreme example of giving, the Lord Jesus Christ. He spoke of three things.

1. His wealth.   Before Christ entered the lowly state of human life in the incarnation, He had lived in all of the wealth of heavenly splendor. He was equal in power, glory, honor, and wisdom with the Father. Though rich in divine power, He voluntarily accepted human limitations. Though rich in the glories of heaven He voluntarily stepped down to the earth. Though rich in divine honor, He voluntarily embraced the shame and humiliation of the cross. Though rich in the wisdom of heaven, He voluntarily declined to exercise this wisdom. Christ laid aside the use of the heavenly riches, but even in His poverty He was still in a real sense rich.[14] Paul discovered this paradox in his life as

---

[14]Christ in the incarnation did not lay aside any of His divine attributes.

an apostle: "poor, yet making many rich; having nothing, and yet possessing everything" (6:10). The life that the eternal Son of God lived in heaven was desirable in every way, but love brought Him to the earth to reconcile rebellious, undeserving men to the heavenly Father.

2. His poverty.   From His home in heaven Christ came into a far country. "When the time had fully come, God sent His Son, born of a woman, born under the law" (Gal. 4:4). What a tremendous step down! Yet not only did He become man for us but He became poor for us also. Jesus' earthly life was not the life He had lived in heaven. He did not even have as much comfort as the birds and the foxes (Matt. 8:20; Luke 9:58). He became poor in all things that we call wealth—poor in the goods of this world, poor in position, poor in reputation and prestige. He lived the life of a servant, and His life ended "in the absolute naked poverty of the cross"[15] (Phil. 2:5-11).

3. His gift of reconciling grace.   The poverty of the Lord was for the purpose of making us truly rich. All that Christ endured—the bearing of our sorrows and our sins and the tasting of our pain and our death—was to make us rich in God.

How does He enrich us? Not, of course, by making us millionaires. What the apostle had in mind was real wealth. It consisted of faith, love, peace with God, and the power of the Holy Spirit. None other than the grace of Christ, which has reconciled us to God, so works to produce all of these. Sharing in the wonderful riches of God's reconciling grace—demonstrated in Jesus who gave Himself freely and fully for us—is the basis for the ministry of giving.

All Christians, like the Corinthians, have been reconciled to God through the lowliness, poverty, and suffering of Christ. That is grace and is the example and inspiration for all Christian giving.

III. THE SENDING OF THE FUND ORGANIZERS
(8:16-24)

Paul had asked for gifts of the Corinthians to relieve the distress of the poor Christians at Jerusalem. With finesse he now proceeded to organize the administrative details of his proposed plan to help the Christians at Jerusalem.

---

[15]C.K. Barrett, *The Second Epistle to the Corinthians* (Harper's New Testament Commentaries), p. 223.

He made every effort to avoid any suspicion of fraud or of personal profit being derived from the collection. He promised to use three trusted Christians to organize and administer the fund in Corinth. In recommending these men he in particular noted their qualifications and indicated how they were to be received.

A. Their Identification (8:16-19,22)

1. Titus (8:16-17). The believers at Corinth knew this man well, and he knew them and their circumstances. But more than that, God was kindling in the heart of Titus a concern to help the Christians at Jerusalem. Paul had appealed to him to assist the Corinthians in bringing to completion the collection (8:6). As time passed, there was no need to ask him. He was eager to go. When Paul approached him again about the matter, he found Titus ready to offer his services in Corinth. It seems that God kindled an enthusiasm in him. Titus did not only have interest in the proper handling of the funds; but God, too, so it seems, had ignited an enthusiasm in his heart to see the Corinthians. It was their money that Titus was hoping to collect, but he was interested in more than their money. He had "the same concern" for them as Paul did. The love that God sheds abroad in our hearts inspires concern and affection for others.

2. The brother (8:18-19). Along with Titus would go "the brother." The identity of this man is unknown. He might have been Luke. Acts 16:10 and 17:1 reveal that Luke was with Paul at Philippi where he could have stayed on for some time. It is just possible that he took a leading role in building up the churches in Macedonia and he would have been an appropriate delegate to assist in carrying the contributions to Jerusalem. Whoever the brother was he was a man of influence and standing. He was highly esteemed in the churches for his preaching and had been chosen by the churches to accompany Paul with the offering to Jerusalem.

3. A third brother (8:22). Accompanying Titus and the brother would be a third delegate. He, too, is unnamed and is designated simply as "our brother." As verse 23 indicates, this brother also was a representative of the churches. Perhaps he was a personal friend of Paul's, possibly Timothy or Apollos. Anyway, to insure him of a proper reception Paul informed the church that he was dependable. This brother had proved in many matters and on many occasions to be zealous. Even now he was more so because of his great confidence that the Corinthians would give willingly and generously.

B. Their Credentials (8:20, 21, 23)

The coming of Titus and his two approved colleagues was more than a financial mission. Their responsibility in organizing the fund was the work of the gospel. There was to be no room for suspecting underhanded dealings or careless administration. The main reason for the careful administration of the fund is stated in verse 20: "We want to avoid any criticism of the way we administer this liberal gift." Any suspicion of dishonesty or blame for inefficiency would have hindered this ministry.

The apostle had a good plan, but he knew that his plan was no better than the men who would administer it. He chose three men who had excellent credentials and who would stand up to any test. They were men who were respected and trusted. Titus, the leader in organizing the fund, was an intimate friend of Paul's. He had been to Corinth on two or more occasions and thus was a fellow worker with Paul in the ministry to the Corinthians. The two companions of Titus were representatives of the churches and had been recognized as able leaders in the church. Their lives reflected the glory of Christ. By discharging faithfully their work of love and service they brought praise to their Savior.

Every precaution was taken by Paul to avoid any charge of misappropriating funds. In no way was he guilty of dishonesty, but he wished to be guiltless in the eyes of men as well as in the eyes of God. Whatever activity he engaged in he desired that it be deemed honorable by both God and man. His scrupulous care in the handling of the money was only wisdom.

As Paul did, we who handle money in trust should take every step, not only to be absolutely honest but also to protect our personal reputation. It is needless to put our good name on the line and jeopardize our reputation. Let us take precautions to safeguard our integrity so that we may bring honor to the cause of Christ that we serve.

C. Their Reputation (8:24)

The Corinthians were urged to receive the delegates. His appeal to the faithful at Corinth to complete the collection was threefold. First, it would show the delegates proof of their love. That would give an outward demonstration that their love was genuine. Second, it would make clear that Paul's great confidence in them was not presumptuous but fully justified. What if the delegates came and found that it was untrue? The apostle could have been thought to have presumed too much. It was just possible that he would have been branded a deceiver. Third, all the churches would hear from the delegates what the Corinthian church did about the collection. Whatever the Corinthian church did or did not do would be made known to other churches. Would Christians at Corinth fail to live up to the high expectations of all? The challenge was that they show proof not only of their love but also all that Paul had said about them.

IV. CONCLUSION

The church is a community of reconciliation and a fellowship in which the ministering to the needs of others has an honored place. The collection project which Paul organized among his missionary churches for the relief of the Jerusalem Christians was an eloquent witness to this truth. His project taught a lesson in community and reconciliation: The Gentile believers were fully part of the church and a lesson in giving; acts of charity among Christians had high value.

The apostle exhorted the Christian community at Corinth to send aid to Jerusalem out of genuine concern for other believers. Their sharing in the collection was not to be a matter of coercion but a matter of their own free will. The Macedonian Christians were an outstanding example by their enthusiastic, spontaneous, sincere participation in the ministry. These Christians' willingness to give was the direct result of and witness to their commitment to Christ. So Christ was the supreme example of giving and was to be the controlling motivation for all Christian service.

The ministry of reconciliation finds its ground and source in Christ's ministry of giving. Being rich, Christ voluntarily became poor so that through His poverty we could be enriched. Without His sacrificial gift we would still be in our poverty of alienation and estrangement from God and from one another. By Christ's coming into the world God has revealed that He is not closed to needs. In Jesus He shared in our weakness, sorrow, and affliction and spent Himself in giving relief to men and reconciling them. Therefore, through His ministry of giving Christ has made us spiritually wealthy and at-one-with God. But also He has committed to us the ministry of reconciliation, which calls for sacrificial activity on the part of the whole church, indeed every Christian.

If the local congregation is to reach out with the gospel at home and abroad, the members must be committed to this ministry of giving. Of course there are things other than money that are needed by the church. Those not having money to give may be able to give something else. Giving should not be seen as a burden and should not become a substitute for other kinds of Christian service, but it is the responsibility of every Christian to participate in the ministry of giving.

9

The True Spirit of Giving

2 Corinthians 9:1-15

The apostle Paul was by no means certain that the Corinthian Christians would give liberally to the collection for the saints in Jerusalem. The matter of the collection had been put before the Corinthians at an earlier time (8:10); but due to troubles which had arisen in the church, it had been laid aside. After the difficulties had been resolved, there was not, so it seems, strong commitment to completing the project. Some among them must have been unwilling givers, desiring to shelve the whole matter and forget it. Their basic weakness, it appears, was that they had not learned the lesson of liberality, which called for the giving of themselves and their money in the service of others.

The collection was a "test" for the Corinthians (8:8, 24; 9:13). The test was never purely the financial aspect, which could have been measured in dollars and cents. What was fundamental was the giver's attitude: "Each man should give what he has decided in his heart to give, not reluctantly or under compulsion, for God loves a cheerful giver" (9:7). If the money were given and received with joy, it would unite Jewish and Gentile Christians. As a single community they could give thanks to God (9:12-14).

In speaking of this gift of money Paul used words like *service, fellowship, blessing,* and *grace*. For him the gift proved the reality of the love that bound all Christians together. The churches in Macedonia manifested exactly the right spirit: "...their overflowing joy and their extreme poverty welled up in rich generosity. ...they gave as much as they were able, and even beyond their ability..." (8:2, 3). Indeed, Christ was the model of giving par excellence: "Though he was rich, yet for your sakes he became poor" (8:9).

The apostle wanted the Corinthians, prompted by love, to give freely and willingly. The truth was that it was their duty to minister to the needs of the mother church in Jerusalem.

With this in mind, we turn to the contents of this chapter in which Paul explains the spirit that is basic to the Christian ministry of giving.

I. GIVING WITHOUT COMPULSION (9:1-5)

The Jerusalem Christians were in desperate need. The apostle was not about to leave the Corinthians' participation in this charitable ministry to chance. This ministry was a privilege of every Christian whose financial resources would allow them to participate. So Paul intensified his appeal for help. His interest was not to coerce the Corinthians but to get them to cooperate.

A. It Was Not Necessary for Him to Write About the Fund (9:1-2)

The reason for his confidence was that at one time they had been enthusiastic about the fund. Their zeal had waned, and now the apostle was still in doubt about their bringing the collection to its completion. Tactfully he acknowledged that it was superfluous to remind them to provide funds for the Christians at Jerusalem.

1. An earlier effort. The past performance of the believers at Corinth was commendable. At an earlier time they had been eager to contribute to the collection and to discharge this ministry. As already noted, the Macedonian example was a basis of Paul's appeal to Corinthian generosity. This time it was not to the example of others that Paul appealed but to the past performance of the Corinthian Christians. Their response when the collection was first introduced at Corinth reflected a keen interest on their part. They were sensitive to the needs of the Judean Christians and ready to minister to their needs.

It is easy in an affluent society such as ours to become callous to human needs. It is easy in our little private worlds of comfort and plenty to build around us walls of selfish indifference. Such walls need to be torn down in the life of every Christian and in the life of the church. The word of reconciliation calls us not only to proclaim the forgiveness of sin through the death and resurrection of Jesus Christ but also to reach out a hand of sympathy and help to the hungry, the poor, the homeless, and the jobless. The reconciling love of Jesus flows through channels of compassion and generosity but not through walls of selfishness and indifference.

2. An earlier enthusiasm. The Macedonian Christians had heard of the zeal of the Corinthians. An enthusiastic beginning had been made at Corinth the previous year. Paul had boasted to them about the eagerness of the Corinthians to share in the collection. The zeal and readiness of the Corinthians had stirred up the Macedonians and stimulated them to give.[1] The Corinthians had begun so well, but now their enthusiasm waned. Learning of that, Paul must have been shocked more than anyone. He did not want his boast to be proven an empty one. An unkind person might have said that Paul had twisted the truth to get the Macedonians to contribute to the fund and thus branded him as a deceiver.

The fact was that Paul made it a habit of thinking the best of his people, and certainly the Corinthians were no exception. They had made a good start, but how tragic it would have been for them to be found unwilling and unready to minister to the needs of their fellow Christians in Jerusalem. That would not happen if Paul could prevent it. Not that he was prepared to resort to psychological tricks and manipulation, as some have in fund raising, but he did take steps to insure the completion of the collection.

B. He Sent Delegates to Assist Them (9:3-5)

There were two reasons that prompted this action.

1. To avoid embarrassment. It was possible that Paul would make another visit to Corinth and that some Macedonians would accompany him. What if the Corinthians did not complete the collection? This would be embarrassing. The Macedonians had heard all the boasting from Paul and so he would be put to shame. The Corinthians, too, would be disgraced. Their failure to complete the collection would compromise their reputation as well as Paul's. After all what could either Paul or they say in the face of such a poor response? If the Co-

---

[1] The phrase "most of them" (*tous pleionas*) does not suggest that some of the Macedonians were still unwilling to share in the collection but that the example of the Corinthians had stirred up more in other places to take part, including particular congregations in Macedonia.

rinthians cooperated with the men Paul sent to assist them in raising the funds, then no one would be embarrassed.

2. To avoid the appearance of pressure from him. Titus and his two companions had been sent not to force the Corinthians to give but to prompt the completion of the fund. What the apostle sought from the Corinthian church was a genuine gift and not something that had to be wrung from them. He wanted them to give in a generous rather than a grudging spirit. If he visited Corinth and they had not gotten the collection together for the destitute Jerusalem Christians, he might have had to make a strong appeal. Rather than their giving on the spur of a moment, he wanted them to give thoughtfully. He sought a gift that was an expression of divine grace and their generosity. Their gift was to be more than money. It would be seen, as someone has said, as "a visible sign of invisible grace."

The mission of Titus and of the two unnamed brothers was to influence the Corinthians to provide the funds promptly so that they would not have to be collected at the last moment. Then when Paul arrived, they could present "a generous gift." There would be no need of pressure from him. That would be to their credit and a sign of God's grace at work. By their gift they would have ministered to the unfortunate and would have expressed to their Jewish brethren at Jerusalem God's reconciling love. It was because God so loved the world that He gave His only Son. The finest gifts are always given thoughtfully and deliberately out of a generous heart.

II. GIVING WITH THE RIGHT ATTITUDE (9:6-9)

Giving gives rise to blessings—blessings to those to whom we give and a return of blessings to ourselves. The Corinthians needed to learn that by giving they enriched themselves. They feared, it appears, that if they were generous, they might suffer later. That was the wrong attitude for them to have had. So Paul went on to reinforce the importance of the right spirit in giving.

A. The Law of Giving (9:6)

The laws of nature were used by Paul to illustrate the Christian law of giving. The farmer reaped as he sowed. If he grudgingly sowed a few seeds, he reaped a scant crop; but if he sowed generously, he reaped bountifully. Jesus said: "...the measure you give will be the measure you receive" (Matt. 7:2, Phillips). This is the law that operates in Christian giving. Consequently the gifts bestowed by Christians to relieve the distress of the needy and support the ministry of reconciliation must not be understood as a throwing away of money. It is an investment, just as grain is sown to yield its return. The appeal is not to a selfish motive. There is no endorsement here of the run-of-the-mill affluence theology. What this teaches is that God has so designed giving that it is regulated and rewarded by the law of harvest. The experience of nature teaches us that this is God's method. Seeds sown will multiply. Sowing seeds of generosity will give returns. The fact is that we do not lose by giving; it comes back to us in one form or another. Many believers can testify to the reality of this in the spiritual realm of Christian experience.

However, Jesus urged us to give without expecting any return. Even so, He never condemned the expectation that sacrifice for His sake would be rewarded. No one will lose his reward if he so much as gives a cup of cold water in Jesus' name (Matt. 10:42). The rewards for generosity are real. Just as God's laws prosper the wise farmer, so do God's laws in the spiritual realm prosper the wise Christian steward. The Christian who sows with a generous hand is certain of a continual, expanding harvest. He sows with only one thing in mind, that of blessings—blessings, praises to God; blessings, benefactions to men; return blessings to himself.[2]

Of course, our returns may not be the same in kind. The apostle Paul had no intention to commercialize and to materialize our giving. Dividends for our generosity may not be material rewards at all. The returns on genuine Christian giving do insure wealth, not however, in material things but in the heart and in the spirit. The generous Christian is certain to be rich in love, in goodness, in friends, and towards God. The great harvest for him will come at the end of the present world order (Matt. 13:39; 25:26) when he appears before the judgment seat of Christ that he may receive what is due him (5:10; Gal. 6:8-9; Eph. 6:8; Col. 3:24). The miserly sower will reap little, but the generous one much. The law of harvest will remain. Each of us will reap what we have sown.

B. The Heart of the Giver

For the apostle true giving was not impulsive but deliberate. It was not due to compulsion but to pleasure. According to Paul, to gain blessings giving must be:

1. Purposeful.   Each Christian at Corinth needed to sow in light of the law of harvest. If he gave generously to the fund for the Jewish brethren, he could ex-

---

[2]R.C.H. Lenski, *Interpretation of First and Second Corinthians*, p. 1170.

pect to reap a bountiful harvest. Whatever a Christian gave should be due to his own decision. No one was to present his gift reluctantly nor because of any compulsion, whether love of praise or the fear of embarrassment. It was left solely to each believer's choice based on responsible stewardship. Having made the decision as to the amount to give, he ought to have adhered to it. Each one must give as he had purposed in his heart.

Christians still choose freely what they want to give, but how much should they give? The amount must be determined by their ability and by the promptings of the Holy Spirit. Many Christians sensitive to the Holy Spirit have been led to give more than a tenth. The need is always great, and the church never seems to have more money than it needs to support the work of the kingdom of God. Giving is a vehicle of love and ministry. In fact, it is a vehicle of reconciliation.

2. Cheerful. "God loves a cheerful giver." This literally means a "hilarious giver." Such a Christian greets the opportunity to give with joy, but it is certain that he is filled with God's love that has healed his brokenness and restored him to fellowship with the Creator. A profound connection exists between love and joy. Both grow out of God's liberating and reconciling grace. One is the test of the genuineness of the other. The man who truly loves is also a cheerful man. The man who truly is cheerful is also one who loves. God's love shed abroad in the human heart by the Holy Spirit prompts us to give gladly.

A mark of cheerfulness, as Paul reminded us, is free, purposeful wholehearted giving. One who gives with that kind of spirit "God loves." This implies that God will reward him. He has no fear that sacrificial giving will work a hardship on him later, nor does he have any regret for what he has given. He finds joy, satisfaction, and enjoyment in giving.

C. Confidence in God's Unlimited Generosity (9:8-9)

All wealth, spiritual and material, comes from God. God is able to reward and is the source of blessings for all who trust Him. Even in this life God's provisions are more than adequate. This is made clear by Paul himself: "God is able to make all grace abound to you, so that in all things at all times, having all that you need, you will abound in every good work." God's purpose, however, for increasing our resources is to enable us to respond to the needs of others. What God gives to His people is not intended for selfish enjoyment; but rather that we "will abound in every good work." God gives so that we can give to others. He is generous with His blessings so that we can minister to those in need.

No one should assume that Paul taught that a Christian is assured of a high standard of living. His own experience proved that this was not true. The life that he faced was a hard one, but as a minister of reconciliation he learned to accept a lowly station, even poverty, for Christ's sake. Without any complaint the apostle spoke of adverse circumstances in which he found himself from time to time. Noteworthy are two particular passages:

> I have known hunger and thirst and have often gone without food; I have been cold and naked (2 Cor. 11:27).
>
> I know what it is to be in need, and I know what it is to have plenty. I have learned the secret of being content in any and every situation, whether well-fed or hungry, whether living in plenty or in want (Phil. 4:12).

Though God offers no guarantees that we will live in affluence, He is able to make us "abound in every good work." Giving is only one of the good works. God's grace supplies us with a sufficiency, and we should not hesitate to dispense it through all kinds of good works and generous acts towards others. Whatever good work is required, God's grace is sufficient for it. This truth challenges us to step out with the assurance that divine grace makes us capable of ministering to the needs of others. Our sufficiency is through God's supply. Resources are needed to give, to help, and to minister. God is sufficient. The problem is not with God, but with us. "God is able to make all grace abound" to us. Here is a challenge for us to act on this promise and to rely on His supplying us with ample means so that we may abound in whatever good work is required.

The blessings of God provide the means for great works of generosity. The Christian does not lose by being generous. Psalm 112:9, which Paul cited, stresses the blessedness of giving: "He has scattered abroad his gifts to the poor, his righteousness endures for ever." The Psalmist understood that the righteous man is liberal toward the poor and the needy as the Corinthians were being asked to be. This kind of man does not give a pittance but presents a goodly gift. His giving is generous even as God's is. Such a man's righteousness, which is his good works and more specifically his generosity, "endures for ever." When "this age" finally gives away to eternity, the Godly man's works—the fruit and the evidence of his faith—will not disappear. On that day the divine verdict will be: "I tell you the truth, whatever you did for one of the least of these brothers of mine, you did for me" (Matt. 25:40). There is a reward waiting for Christians who share with others some of the provisions God has given to them. God will give to all believers, including the Corinthians, an eternal blessing for their generosity.

III. GIVING: ITS CAUSE AND EFFECT (9:10-15)

God's resources are inexhaustible. The apostle assured the Corinthians that their participation in the collection would benefit them and the Christians in Jerusalem. But more than that their generosity would cause thanksgiving to abound to God. It goes without saying, giving has a proper cause and effect.

A. Its Cause (9:10-11)

Divine providence stands behind the whole process of sowing and reaping. The farmer must put the seed in the earth and gather the harvest, but it is God who multiplies what is planted and gives a bountiful return. Rain and snow come down from heaven and water the earth and cause the seed to germinate and sprout. God, therefore, causes the work of the sower to prosper and his seed to bear much fruit.

This is a law, but it is not limited to the world of nature. "The same law of an increasing return operates in the life of faith."[3] On this basis the apostle assured the Corinthian Christians that generous action coupled with a right attitude would be blessed by God in two ways. First, God would cause their generosity to produce a splendid spiritual harvest. By their giving generously to the collection, God would enlarge their harvest of righteousness. The Corinthians' return would be a spiritual harvest. God willed to provide the increase of the fruits for such deeds as giving to the collection; but the bounty of their spiritual blessings would be in terms of their generosity. So it is with us in our spiritual life. Greater generosity in giving and in other religious deeds yield greater spiritual blessings.

Second, God would enrich the Corinthians so that they could always be generous. They would be rewarded for their gifts of money by a God-given enrichment. Their giving to the collection would issue from hearts rich in generosity. God's grace would make them richer "in every way," that is, both spiritually and materially. The purpose of such enrichment was not primarily for the benefit of the Christians at Corinth, but so that they could "be generous on every occasion." God would fill their lives with His grace and generosity so that they could minister to the needs of others and through their deeds of liberality produce a great harvest of benevolence. God blesses us so that we are able to be generous. Selfish greed that hoards earthly riches should have no place in our hearts. God wills that we share with the less fortunate

---

[3]James Reid, *The Second Epistle to the Corinthians*, (Interpreter's Bible), p. 378.

some of our blessings. That is why God multiplies our blessings, even in material things.

B. Its Effects (9:12-15)

According to Paul giving would have wonderful effects from three different perspectives.

1. On others (9:12-13).   First, it would meet needs of the Jerusalem Christians. Those Christians were in desperate need. "This service" (literally, "ministry") would relieve their distress. The Corinthians must not let their Jerusalem brethren suffer want. They had an opportunity for ministry.

Second, it would increase the Jerusalem church's thanksgiving to God. The giving encouraged by Paul would do more than relieve human need. It would cause the hearts of the poor of Jerusalem to be filled with thanksgiving to God. Apparently the Jerusalem church, almost entirely Jewish, had been suspicious of the Corinthians' loyalty and doubted whether they were Christians at all. The poor saints, benefiting from the gifts of the Corinthians, would set aside such doubts and thanksgiving would rise from their hearts and lips to God for the generosity of the Corinthian church. Such a response would have been appropriate.

Christian giving produces thanksgiving to God. The apostle himself received gifts of money from the Christians at Philippi. He described their gift as "a fragrant offering, an acceptable sacrifice, pleasing to God" (Phil. 4:18). Thanksgiving redounded to God for the generosity of the Philippians. Truly their gifts were "a fragrant offering" and "pleasing to God."

Third, it would be a practical proof for the Jewish Christians of the Corinthians' loyalty to the gospel. Those in Jerusalem who would benefit from the collection would not simply praise God for the cash gift. Paul identified two particular reasons why they would be prompted to praise God:

(1) For obedience which accompanied the Corinthians' confession of the gospel of Christ. Their confession of faith in the gospel would not be a matter of words only but also of true obedience to God. Their gift to the needy brethren would guarantee the reality of their Christianity. The Jerusalem Christians would see that indeed the Corinthians had experienced God's reconciling grace and love. The Corinthian generosity would show that their response to the gospel was genuine. That would prompt the Jerusalem Christians to glorify God. The racial barrier between Jewish and Gentile believers would be overcome. Racial barriers are still very real. Through Jesus Christ

they can be set aside and reconciliation realized. Genuine Christian love can dissolve both prejudice and antagonism and build a bridge of fellowship between those once alienated from one another.

(2) For the Corinthians' "generosity in sharing [*koinōnia,* "fellowship"] with them." By contributing to the collection the Corinthians would share even in the trials of the Jewish Christians. All Christians, whether Jew or Gentile, belonged to the same fellowship—"the communion of saints." This was a spiritual fellowship, in fact, an intimate fellowship of believers with Christ and with each other. Christians were bound together and still are in a mutual fellowship. When the Jerusalem Christians received the collection, Paul anticipated that they would praise God. Their praise would not simply be for the gift of money from Corinth but for the great Christian fellowship that it expressed. Sending aid to Jerusalem was a genuine expression of the Gentiles' fellowship with Christ and with all other Christians. A bridge of fellowship would be built between Jewish and Gentile Christians. Such a bridge should be constructed wherever cultural, racial, or any other kind of prejudice separates Christians so that there may be reconciliation, fellowship, love, and understanding among God's people.

2. On the giver (9:14).　The collection was more than the means of ministering to a need. It would turn "distant strangers into eager and earnest friends."[4] What would be the effect of the Corinthians' generosity? First, it would cause the Jerusalem Christians to pray for them. The needs of those Christians would have been supplied. As a result they would long to see the Corinthians, but direct fellowship was not possible since Jerusalem and Corinth were too far apart. Though they could not embrace the Corinthians and thank them personally, they would express their gratitude by praying for their benefactors.

Second, it would cause the saints in Jerusalem to be aware of the grace of God given to the faithful in Corinth. Since their distress would have been relieved by Corinthian resources, naturally the Jerusalem Christians would have strong affection for their friends in Corinth. This would have been human enough. However, the true significance of the Corinthians' generosity would be outside of themselves, and would be found in "the surpassing grace of God." Their generosity would be a mark of God's grace. This would be the main motivation for Jewish Christians' desire to see the Corinthians. Those who lived in the grace of God would long to meet their Corinthian friends who

---

[4]R.H. Strachan, *The Second Epistle of Paul to the Corinthians,* (The Moffatt New Testament Commentaries), p. 144.

also lived in the grace of God. They would feel strong affection for them because of this excelling grace of God. This is the proper motivation for Christian generosity and is the foundation for Christian love and fellowship.

3. On the Divine Giver (9:15).   Paul exclaimed: "Thanks be to God for his indescribable gift!" God's gift, precious and beyond description, was Jesus Christ, the supreme example of the self-giving of God and the source and inspiration of all Christian giving. God "did not spare his own Son but gave him up for us all" (Rom. 8:32). What a marvelous gift! No wonder the apostle burst out in praise as he brought to a close his exposition of sacrificial giving. It is God's gift of His Son that reconciles men to God and brings them together in Christian fellowship. In giving, our thoughts should be turned to God's indescribable gift, Jesus Christ.

IV. CONCLUSION

Christianity began with God's gift of His Son. What God has done in us and for us He has done in Christ. Therefore Christian giving is not something which originated in ourselves. It is the gift of God. This was precisely why the apostle picked up the great theme, "the surpassing grace of God given to you" and went on to speak of God's indescribable gift (9:15). Our giving, all of our good works, all of the fruits produced by them are but part of God's grace. The maximum expression of God's grace is what He accomplished in His Son. Christ gave Himself freely and fully for us. All Christians would do well to compare their attitudes and practice of sharing with that of our Savior. His sacrificial life reflects the true spirit of Christian giving and is the ground of our reconciliation with God and with one another.

Any proper understanding of Christian generosity must discern that its roots are in divine grace. The apostle made this clear when he said:

> For you know the grace of our Lord Jesus Christ, that though he was rich, yet for your sakes he became poor, so that you through his poverty might become rich (2 Cor. 8:9).

He encouraged the believers at Corinth to provide for the poor of Jerusalem. His object was not merely the relief of personal suffering. He saw the collection as an opportunity to promote mutual affection and the closest fellowship between the Jewish and Gentile Christians and to heal the wounds of alienation within the body of Christ. Their contributions to the relief fund were a sign of grace.

Prompted by divine love, the Corinthians were to share their bounty with others. As sown seed will multiply, they were assured by Paul that their generosity would give unlimited returns. Any practical minded man would have been enticed by such compounded interest. But did Paul teach that Christians' increase would always be in worldly substance? Surely God has blessed some immensely with an abundance of material wealth, but prosperity is no sure sign of God's blessings and spiritual growth. It may be nothing more than a snare of the devil to entrap the Christian and destroy his relationship with Christ. Wealth has its place, but Paul warned us of the inevitable spiritual disaster of materialism:

> People who want to get rich fall into temptation and a trap and into many foolish and harmful desires that plunge men into ruin and destruction (1 Tim. 6:9).

Some today are proclaiming a "gospel of prosperity" in which supposedly the good life leads to unlimited material wealth. Such people solicit funds with the promise: "Give and the Lord will give you more in return." It is true that the Lord does bless His people who give sacrificially, but there is no guarantee that the returns can be measured in dollars and cents. Anyway, God has already blessed us, and He has been doing it for years. We can never repay Him fully and not even partially for "his indescribable gift." The fact remains that we should be good stewards of what God has given us and use what we have for the sake of Christ and for the sake of humanity.

10

A Defense of the Ministry

2 Corinthians 10:1—11:33

Reconciliation between Paul and the Corinthians did not eliminate all sources of tension. In the last four chapters of 2 Corinthians he presented a firm defense of his ministry. These chapters consist of a sharp rebuke, not of the whole Christian community at Corinth but of those whom Paul described as "false apostles, deceitful workers, masquerading as apostles of Christ" (11:13). They had invaded the community and were sowing seeds of discord among the Christians.

The apostle disputed these troublemongers' claims to be "servants of righteousness" (11:15) and mockingly called them "super-apostles" (11:5; 12:11). These false apostles were opposing the gospel of God and the truth of Christ as proclaimed by Paul (11:7, 10). Precisely what their teaching was we cannot now tell. Paul gave very little information about them beyond the fact that they were Jews (11:22). They must have claimed to be more Jewish and superior spiritually to the apostle or his converts. Likely they prided themselves in keeping the law, a foremost distinguishing mark of a Jew, and condemned Paul for his unwillingness to introduce to the Corinthians the Mosaic law as being essential to salvation. From all indications the Corinthian agitators represented a Jewish-Christian movement determined to make the law indispensable and superior to the gospel.

The situation called for stern words. The troublemakers denied Paul's authority and integrity and questioned the reliability of his message of reconciliation through faith. Over and over he encouraged the pursuit of peace. "Live in harmony with one another" (Rom. 12:16). "Make every effort to keep the unity of the Spirit through the bond of peace" (Eph. 4:3). "Let us therefore make every effort to do what leads to peace" (Rom. 14:19). However, he did not push "peace at any price." He urged the Christians at Rome "to watch out for those who cause divisions and put obstacles in your way, contrary to the teaching you have learned. Keep away from them" (Rom. 16:17). He would have nothing to do with the accommodation of error under the cloak of reconciliation. Distortion of basic doctrine required discipline and correction because purity in faith was essential to unity.

Inevitably all church controversies fall into two categories: substantive (centered in ideas and doctrine) and interpersonal (due to personality clashes). The conflict reflected in chapters 10-13 was of the substantive type.[1] Paul defended the gospel of grace and his ministry. Yet in his stern moments he interwove into what he wrote a disarming humility and expressed a deeper love than what may be thought at first. At times "sternness" in love is necessary in working through painful and troublesome problems. Certainly this was true in Paul's defense of the true gospel and his ministry against the so-called "super-apostles."

I. HIS REPLY TO THE CHARGE OF COWARDICE (10:1-6)

Word had reached Paul that certain intruders into the Corinthian church were seeking to sabotage his character and ministry. They sought to build up their own reputations by destroying Paul's reputation as a servant of Christ. Their aim was to win for themselves the Corinthians' love by destroying their affection for Paul. Nothing would have pleased them more than for the apostle's person and ministry to have been held in contempt by the Corinthians. He began his defense by appealing to the Corinthians on the basis of "the

---

[1]As well as overcoming conflict, reconciliation leads to it. This was the experience of Jesus. He lived among his own people and ministered to all kinds of sinful people, but He found Himself in conflict with the Pharisees and others. His life and teachings judged their sins, their stress on the externals of religion and their national hopes. It should come as no surprise that God's act of reconciliation does in a sense create conflict. Those who accept God's reconciling grace and those who resist it find little common ground on which to construct a harmonious relationship.

meekness and gentleness of Christ." A man, meek and gentle, would not lose his temper or grow impatient. Paul determined to be a Christian in vindicating himself against the charges of his critics.

A. No Imposing Presence (10:1)

Apparently his opponents had said that he was humble in their presence but a bully when he was absent, that is, when he was face to face with those who would stand up to him, he was a timid coward and unimpressive, but at a distance in writing letters he was bold and strong. Because of this a saying concerning Paul began to circulate at Corinth: "His letters are weighty and forceful, but in person he is unimpressive and his speaking amounts to nothing" (2 Cor. 10:10). Noticeably the pomp and show of the adversaries were absent from Paul's ministry. Humility was nothing but cowardice for them. They failed to discern that humility was vital to the service of the humble Christ. In contrast, Paul's ministry was characterized by "the meekness and gentleness of Christ." He did not want his Corinthian friends to force him to adopt a different attitude. Above all he desired to show how a man would live if Christ was living in him. Personal impressiveness and magnetism, which the "super-apostles" associated with the spiritual life, were not motivations for Paul's ministry. He was eager to follow the example of his Lord and give a genuine demonstration of Christlikeness. But he was not about to take the accusation of his opponents "lying down." Evil and evil men had to be resisted.

The ministry of reconciliation is a spiritual warfare; but as Paul did, it must be carried out in a spirit of humility. Pride and self-will have no place in this kind of ministry. The humble servant of God has had his pride and self-will crucified and the model for his lifestyle is "the meekness and gentleness of Christ."

B. Not Guided by Worldly Standards (10:2-3)

As we have noted, the false teachers at Corinth did not count humility a virtue. So they called Paul a coward, mistaking his meekness for weakness. The apostle had confidence in God and the gospel, but this confidence did not make him pushy and overbearing as his opponents were. But their charge of cowardice was not the end of it. These carnal men also accused him of worldliness and suspected that he lacked genuine spirituality. The charge, therefore, was that he lived "by the standards of this world."

Paul affirmed that he lived "in the world." As a Christian his circumstances were those common to human experience. He was not exempt from conflict, difficulty, suffering, and temptation. Many of the problems that he faced were problems of the world of men and women in his day. He was tempted, like other people, to yield to his appetites and to use under-handed means to accomplish noble ends. He did not, however, succumb to a worldly spirit, nor did he lose his spiritual balance or awareness of being a servant of Christ. As a herald of reconciling grace the apostle fought fiercely in the cause of Christ against the forces of evil. But he did not "wage war as the world does." In his ministry he did not use the worldly weapons of cunning and deceit. He never lost sight of his mission of reconciliation. No matter how strong the temptation, he never resorted to carnal means to accomplish this mission. He was "in the world," but he lived and ministered "according to the Spirit."

C. Fighting with God's Powerful Weapons (10:4-6)

Like his war, Paul's weapons were not worldly, but they were "divine power to tear down strongholds." Worldly weapons were impressive, but the apostle's weapons were powerful—though not necessarily perceived that way by men. They were not weak, carnal weapons of man. They were spiritual and were instruments of great power. With these weapons he could destroy strongholds—carnal notions and false arguments—that defiantly exalted themselves against God and His knowledge revealed in Christ. The troublemakers were guilty of exalting themselves against Christ and the good news that declared that man is saved by grace and grace alone. They were antagonistic toward Paul but more so toward his message of reconciliation. His aim was to bring men's designs, cleverness, and highmindedness into captivity and obedience to Christ. The apostle was ready enough to wage war. He, however, did not fight for himself but for Christ.

This spiritual warfare was not waged by Paul in his own strength. No one saw him bristling with power. He was everything but a powerful, impressive personality. In himself he was weak and just a vessel of clay. His weakness made it sure, as he wrote, "that this all-surpassing power is from God and not from us" (4:7). The success of his ministry could be traced only to God.

The troublemakers at Corinth did not see what they deemed to be signs of strength and power in Paul. For them he was not with it spiritually, but it seems that they imagined themselves to be super-Christians. Paul's concern was not to appear powerful and spiritual as the worldly mind judges power and spirituality. However, there are those who still fail to understand that in the Christian life "we live by faith, not by sight" (5:8). There are no super-

Christians and never have been any, but there are those who have learned, as Paul did, to lean heavily on the Lord and to rely on His power.

II. HIS REPLY TO THE CHARGE OF WEAKNESS AND CONTEMPTIBLE SPEECH (10:7-11)

The intruders were seeking to ruin Paul's work at Corinth. He urged the Corinthians to look at the situation as it really was—not just on the surface. They were judging according to external appearance. It was a poor and inaccurate way to judge. The rival missionaries claimed to be superior to Paul. The apostle's authority as a minister of the gospel was God-given, but the believers at Corinth were prone to accept the false apostles' claims of superiority. To get his friends at Corinth to open their eyes and look, Paul proceeded to point out facts plain to see.

A. His Relationship to Christ (10:7)

By his critics Paul was considered to lack real spiritual credentials and to be nothing more than a coward. That was not the only charge they made. They went on to question whether he was a Christian at all. His response was: "If anyone is confident that he belongs to Christ, he should consider again that we belong to Christ just as much as he." The plain fact was that Paul belonged to Christ as much as anyone making such a boast. No one had any right to deny his standing as a Christian. His opponents had no claim on Christ that he did not have. They had no right to de-christianize him. He belonged to Christ as every Christian does.

Divisions have appeared in churches when those claiming special holiness or spirituality have looked down on their fellow Christians. Churches have been ripped apart when external tests based on appearances rather than on character have been applied in an arrogant, harsh spirit. Real fellowship with Jesus Christ does not make a person look down on his brothers and sisters in the Lord. A true sense of fellowship in Christ gives no room for pride and it heals rather than creates divisions in the church. A prideful Christian thinks that Christ belongs to him rather than that he belongs to Christ.

B. His Authorized Boasting (10:8)

The super-apostles were demeaning Paul. So he felt compelled to boast, but he would boast only in his God-given authority to build up the church in Corinth. He would not be put to shame for he would state the truth and no more. He had been the first evangelist at Corinth. Christ had called him to the ministry of reconciliation and had granted him authority for the building of the Christian fellowship in that city. On the contrary his enemies were using their authority and influence to demolish the church. They created and promoted nasty feelings, strife, enmity, and hatred within the Christian community. It is a fact that anything that destroys the fellowship of believers is sin. Every Christian should therefore apply this test to his conduct: Does what I do tend to build up or tear down the fellowship?

C. His Letters and Speech (10:9-11)

According to the scoffers, when Paul was at a distance, he was forceful; but when present he was weak. In other words, his letters were weighty in substance and powerful in threats, but his personality was feeble and his speaking amounted to nothing. When he came again, they would find that his actions and words were consistent.

There might have been some ground for the charge that his appearance and speech were unimpressive. When he first visited Corinth, he confessed that he came "in weakness and fear, and with much trembling" (1 Cor. 2:3). Plagued with fear and a gnawing sense of incompetence, Paul learned that God's power was made perfect in weakness (12:9) and that when he was weak he was strong (12:10). When he reflected on his ministry, he concluded that when I am weak, God can work through me better because I stand in the way a little less.

Paul was aware of a deep dependence on God. His competence came from God (3:5). It was not by his impressiveness and eloquence but by the power of the Holy Spirit that the gospel gripped the hearts of men and reconciled them to God. Like Paul, every Christian needs to learn that his sufficiency is from God. We may be weak and timid, but we can be strong through the power of the Spirit in declaring the truth. After all is said and done, it is not our own capacity but the good news of reconciliation that breaks through and meets the needs of people.

III. HIS REPLY TO THE CHARGE OF AMBITION
(10:12-18)

The lifestyle of the false apostles stood in contrast to that of Paul. They were in the business of self-advertisement and boasted of their spiritual attainment (10:8, 13, 15, 17, 18). Paul would not degrade himself by stooping to their level.

A. His Rejection of Self-Commendation (10:12)

The aim of the rival apostles was to supplant Paul and gain control of the church at Corinth. So they mocked Paul's humility and spoke highly of themselves. As ambitious and insecure men do, they were blowing their own trumpets. Being aware of their astounding claims, Paul wrote: "We do not dare to classify or compare ourselves with some who commend themselves." They measured their worth by their own standards. By those standards they could be nothing but bright and shining lights in the church. Measuring and commending themselves by self-chosen standards left no doubt that they were unwise. They compared themselves with themselves which was tantamount to the use of no standards at all. That was folly. They had their own little mutual admiration society and had no intention of measuring themselves by Paul's standards for the ministry of reconciliation.

It is always flattering to measure our motives, our goodness, and our ministry by ourselves, but it is blind and false. The true standards are Christ's standards. In light of those we are to measure ourselves. When we do, hopefully it will move us not to self-praise but to the praise of the Savior.

B. His Field of Labor Set by God (10:13-16)

God had assigned Paul a field of ministry—a field that included the Corinthians. His task was to carry the gospel to Corinth. So he had gone to the city under God's guidance and preached to people previously untouched by the gospel. He did not intrude, as his rivals had, into another man's region of missionary work. What he did in Corinth was authorized and blessed by God. If Paul boasted, it was not going to be in terms of what he did but in terms of what God had done through his ministry. His boast was only in the work that God had given him and God's blessings on that work.

As a pioneer missionary the apostle had broken new ground in the city. He declared the wonderful message of reconciliation to those who as yet had not heard it. It was a rule of his not to build on another man's foundation where others had already preached the gospel (Rom. 15:20-21).[2] The passion of evangelism gripped his heart, and his desire was to preach in regions yet unreached by the gospel.

---

[2]Paul made one exception. He did not establish the church in Rome, but he had hope of reaping some harvest in that city by his missionary work (Rom.1:13-14).

Above all the apostle did not want to intrude into someone else's field of labor. But that was what his opponents had done. They had invaded the field of work that God had assigned him and sought to convert the Corinthians to their strange gospel (11:4). They credited themselves with labors of others. It is common today for congregations, even in the same denomination, to compete with one another and to attract members from one church to another. They measure success by their power to persuade Christians to place their membership in another church. They take credit for souls they have not won. This contributes nothing to the triumphs of the gospel. The church, like any other organism, cannot grow by feeding on itself.

C. His Desire for Divine Commendation (10:17-18)

The false apostles commended themselves, boasted in their success and took credit for Paul's work at Corinth. The fact was no Christian should have boasted of his own work much less have taken credit for the successes of others. All the credit belonged to the Lord: "Let him who boasts boast in the Lord." Those troublemongers at Corinth boasted of their success, but Paul warned that man's commendation has no value. It was not those who commend themselves who are spiritual but those whom Christ commends. The judgment of Christ is the final test of a man's character and ministry.

The basis of a man's pride in his Christian service is what the Lord has done. He is never to boast of his own spiritual achievements. Those who claim to be super-Christians, great movers of the church, have missed the point.

IV. HIS PLAYING THE ROLE OF A FOOLISH BOASTER (11:1-12)

Proud and pretentious were the Corinthian agitators. With a sense of spiritual superiority they had entered the Christian community and were preaching strange doctrine. They also attacked its founder, the apostle Paul. To save the church from their destructive influence he felt compelled to defend his ministry. As we have noted, he had insisted that all human boasting was wrong; but to get his Corinthian friends to see the truth, he asked them to bear with a little of his foolish boasting. Because of the desperate situation his folly was necessary. But "Christians have not always been as successful in distinguishing between regrettable and unnecessary folly, regrettable but necessary folly."[3]

A. His Motive (11:2-4)

The apostle turned aside momentarily from boasting to express his concern for the Corinthians. He felt a holy jealousy for the church, but it did not stem from an ulterior motive. He was not anxious about his own reputation or the loss of prestige. What he feared was not that the Corinthians would transfer their loyalty from him to his enemies but that they would be led away from the Christian faith that he had taught them. He was deeply concerned about the spiritual progress of his Corinthian friends. With a God-given jealousy he was jealous for their purity of doctrine and life. Aware that they were inclined to follow the false apostles, Paul reminded them of two facts.

First, he had arranged a wedding contract between the church at Corinth and Christ Himself. "I promised you to one husband, to Christ, so that I might present you as a pure virgin to him." The fact that Paul particularly pointed to "one husband" expressed well the Corinthian problem. They were not satisfied with the "one"—they were attracted to more than one. They were engaged to "one husband"—Jesus Christ—but there was imminent danger of their being unfaithful to Him. Their chaste devotion to Him was in jeopardy. Nothing but the welfare of the church moved Paul to holy jealousy for their single-hearted devotion to Christ and to the gospel. Out of genuine love sprang such concern.

Second, there was an attempt to win the church away from Christ. The missionary intruders, inspired by Satan (11:13-15), were wooing the Corinthians to abandon the Christ whom Paul preached. Deceived by Satanic cunning, the believers at Corinth were behaving as Eve did in Eden and were in deadly peril. These influential opponents preached "another Jesus," "a different spirit,"[4] and "a different gospel." To Paul's dismay his converts were very willing to submit to them. Christianity could be summed up for him in three words: *Jesus, Spirit,* and *gospel.* He had made Jesus and His cross-death the foundation of the church at Corinth. It seems the rival apostles preached Jesus as a divine miracle-worker but little, if any at all, as the suffering servant who reconciles man and restores him to fellowship with God (Isa. 53). These people

---

[3]C.K. Barrett, *The Second Epistle to the Corinthians* (Harper's New Testament Commentaries), p. 271.

[4]Here "a different spirit" was evidently regarded as satanic (11:13-15), but those who believed the gospel Paul preached received the Holy Spirit.

were impressive, claiming to be able to lead the Corinthians into a greater depth in God. After all, the founder of the church had admitted he had weaknesses; he had experienced many troubles and lacked personal magnetism. The new missionaries insisted that where Paul introduced them to Christianity, they could lead them to experience Jesus, the Spirit, and the gospel in a fuller way.

The fact was "a different Jesus," preached by the false apostles, led to "a different gospel," devoid of real reconciling power. Moreover "a different Jesus" introduced "a different spirit" into the church—not the Holy Spirit who was the Spirit of liberty but a satanic spirit that sought to restore the shackles of legalism. Understandably the apostle was disappointed and alarmed. His Corinthian friends were listening to the higher teachers and "putting up with it" easily enough. They had been betrothed to the true Christ and believed the true gospel. Unless they continued in sincere and pure devotion to Christ and the gospel, they were in great peril.

The teachings of the rival apostles are just as deadly today as they were then. Jesus Christ, stripped of His saving grace and viewed merely as a great teacher and miracle-worker, is not the Christ in whom God reconciled the world unto Himself. Jesus, who is declared to be nothing more than a social reformer, the supreme example of morality, and an outstanding spiritual man is not the true Jesus of the Christian faith. This is a rejection of Jesus as the crucified Lord. The result is a different gospel and a different religious experience which is not of the Holy Spirit.

B. His Ministry (11:5-6)

For the first time in this epistle Paul ventured a name for these traveling missionaries who invaded Corinth. They were "super-apostles"—so they claimed. While they thought of themselves as apostles of the highest dignity, they were not apostles at all. They were "false apostles" (11:13-15). Their sense of superiority was denied by Paul: "I do not think that I am the least inferior to those 'super-apostles.'"

The apostle noted two differences between himself and his opponents. First, he was not a trained speaker, for he had not been educated in the techniques of Greek rhetoric. Language skills dedicated to God have their place in the ministry, but the apostle was content with unpretentious speech. He knew, as we do, that the Holy Spirit can work through those who are unskilled in polished oratory.

Second, he was not an amateur in knowledge of the truth of the gospel. That was the knowledge that saved men and that healed broken relationships. That was the knowledge that counted, but that was precisely what the false apostles perverted—the real knowledge seen in Jesus Christ. Paul knew the truth of the gospel not merely by intellectual grasp but also through an experience with the living Christ. Polished eloquence was not Paul's forte, but it was clear to the Corinthians that he was skilled in the knowledge of the truth.

C. His Preaching Without Charge (11:7-12)[5]

The attitude toward remuneration was still another difference between Paul and the opponents. Apparently they demanded and received support from the church (11:20). But the ministry of Paul at Corinth had been sacrificial. He had taken no money from the church. Because of this the super-apostles sought to discredit Paul. Likely they said that this was a sign he did not love and care for the church (verse 11). As well as laboring with his own hands (Acts 18:3), he had received support from other churches so that he would not be a burden. The Corinthians had shown no sign of appreciation. Likely they esteemed him less for his sacrifices. If he considered his preaching worth anything, they thought, it seems, that he would have insisted on the hire of which the laborer is worthy (Luke 10:7). He regretted their ingratitude and misunderstanding. His desire was to give them the good news without cost.

No money had been taken by Paul from the Corinthian church. The apostle, therefore, went on to point out a couple of things. First, he had never been a burden to them. Other churches had provided his support. He had received financial assistance from the Macedonians, especially the Philippians (Phil. 4:14-16) while he ministered in Corinth. The Corinthians had never supported him, but he received money from churches that could hardly spare anything. "I robbed other churches," he told them, "by receiving support from them so as to serve you." He had refused his pay and would continue that practice so that he would not be a burden in any way.

Second, he boasted about ministering for nothing. The church owed more to Paul than to his rivals; he had served the church without charging them a thing. He had no intention of doing otherwise. So the apostle asked: "Why? Because I do not love you?" God knew that he did love the Corinthians. Why did he not accept support? There was nothing essentially wrong with it, but his

---

[5]It is proper to expect a material return for spiritual service (Luke 10:7; 1 Tim. 5:18). At Corinth Paul had foregone that right, but he did not always do this (Phil. 4:16, 17).

rivals would have liked for him to accept pay. They did not want to serve without remuneration. So if Paul changed his policy, they could claim to work on the same terms as he did. As long as he served for nothing, they could not put themselves in the same category with him unless they adopted his practice.

Receiving a material return for ministry is good. It gives ministers freedom for more important spiritual tasks and allows them to devote their time and talents more fully to Christian service, but never should a price-tag be placed on their ministry.

V. HIS CONTRAST WITH THE COUNTERFEIT TEACHERS (11:13-33)

The activities of the Corinthian opponents were divisive. Their spiritual pride, self-advertisement, and grandiose claims promoted friction, animosity, and schism, and had the potential of demolishing the Christian community. Because of that Paul felt compelled to expose them fully and to single out his credentials for ministry.

A. The Character of the Counterfeit Teachers (11:13-20)

The intruders lacked the marks of true servants of Christ. Indeed they were deceivers, as becomes clear from Paul's estimate.

1. They were masquerading as servants of righteousness (11:13-15). From all outward appearance they were doing the work of Christ, but in reality they were "deceitful workmen, masquerading as apostles of Christ." These false apostles put forth every effort to discredit Paul and to destroy his influence and ministry. They were prompted by dishonesty and selfish motives. Their real aim was not to serve Christ but to promote themselves and to capitalize on the gospel. The love of power, success, and prestige was behind their religious masquerade. The apostle was not surprised, for he discerned their master and source of inspiration:

> And no wonder, for Satan himself masquerades as an angel of light. It is not surprising, then, if his servants masquerade as servants of righteousness. Their end will be what their actions deserve (11:14-15).

The opponents dressed up "as apostles of Christ" and "as servants of righteousness," but they were ministers of Satan and advocated righteousness through the works of the law rather than through faith in Christ. These imposters distorted divine grace by which God reconciles man to Himself. What the final outcome would be of their deceitful actions was not in doubt.

Paul, in contrast to these detractors, was prompted by honest and sincere motives and labored in the gospel for the love of God. By Paul's own example we can test whether our Christianity is a reality or a religious masquerade.

2. They were boasting after the flesh (11:16-21a).   The best way that Paul could meet the challenge of his opponents was by boasting. Seeing the peril of the Corinthian church, he sought to beat them at their own game. From a Christian viewpoint he knew that he was making himself a fool. Only under great duress would a Christian parade his own record. To meet the crisis, he had no choice but to become a braggart. Nevertheless it left him unhappy to have to speak not according to the Lord's example but "as a fool."

Turning to his rivals, Paul remarked: "Many are boasting in the ways the world does." Proud they were, boasting of their abilities, position and achievements, but not "in the Lord"—not in what God had graciously done through Jesus Christ to reconcile the world to Himself. They elevated themselves, but not the Christ Paul preached.

The Corinthians were not entirely free of this attitude of superiority. Pride was nothing new at Corinth. Earlier Paul had rebuked them for their supposed superior wisdom (1 Cor. 4:10). Again, from high attitudes they looked down on the apostle and assumed themselves to be wise. With some sarcasm Paul observed that they would gladly put up with his foolish talk. Did they really think themselves to be wise? They had been unwise. Wise people would never have endured the intruders' overbearing, unscrupulous tactics and pompous behavior. That was exactly what the Corinthians had tolerated. "You even put up with anyone who enslaves you or exploits you or takes advantage of you or pushes himself forward or slaps you in the face." The troublemakers bullied the church members and employed any means to get their way. But in contrast to them Paul was not pushy and dictatorial. Therefore with irony he confessed: "To my shame I admit that we were too weak for that!" His presence in Corinth had been described as "weakness" (10:10). Indeed he had been weak when compared with the greed, pride, exploitation, harshness, and violence of the imposters. If these were marks of a servant of Christ, then Paul was a weakling and a miserable failure.

B. The Credentials of the Apostle (11:21b-33)

Since the Corinthians had endured the abuse of the agitators, surely they would tolerate his "speaking as a fool." However, boasting was not something that he looked forward to doing. Blowing his own trumpet was utterly offensive to him, but he had postponed it as long as he could. If the imposters had things to boast about, so did he. If they had to parade their credentials, so did he. As a madman does, he commenced to boast of his position and record, not only matching but also exceeding the claims of the rival missionaries.

1. His credentials as a Jew (11:22-23). He had the same spiritual heritage and ancestry as his opponents. Their background was no more distinguished and noble than his. "Are they Hebrews? So am I. Are they Israelites? So am I. Are they Abraham's descendants? So am I" (11:22). They gloated over their lineage, religious heritage, and aristocracy of birth. So could the apostle. (1) He was a Hebrew. The Hebrews left behind Ur of the Chaldees, settled in the Promised Land, and were the nucleus of a new race. The apostle was a full Jew by descent—a Hebrew born to parents who were both Hebrews (Phil. 3:5). (2) He was an Israelite. The Israelites were the chosen people of God, the covenantal people (Rom. 11:1). His faith had been no other than the faith of people with whom God made a covenant at Mount Sinai. From a religious as well as a racial angle Paul had the same ground for pride as his opponents. (3) He was a descendant of Abraham. God called Abraham and gave him a promise. Paul belonged to the people who were heirs of God's promises. Included in those promises were a people and a redemptive purpose. Through those people all of the families of the earth were to be blessed and finally through them would come the Redeemer through whom God would take the initiative to reconcile fallen man to Himself (5:19).

Whatever his opponents claimed to be, Paul was. He, too, was a pure Hebrew, a member of the nation of Israel and a descendant of Abraham.

2. His credentials as a servant of Christ (11:21-33). Paul's opponents boasted of being special servants of Christ. That he could boast of, too, but he added, "I am more—I am out of my mind to talk like this." Self-praise was a painful assignment for him, but he cited proof of why he was "more" a servant of Christ than the "super-apostles." He had good reasons for making this superior claim. Consider the evidence, the catalogue of his difficulties:

> I have worked much harder, been in prison more frequently, been flogged more severely, and been exposed to death again and again. Five times I received from the

Jews the forty lashes minus one. Three times I was beaten with rods, once I was stoned, three times I was shipwrecked, I spent a night and a day in the open sea, I have been constantly on the move. I have been in danger from rivers, in danger from bandits, in danger from my own countrymen, in danger from Gentiles; in danger in the city, in danger in the country, in danger at sea; and in danger from false brothers. I have labored and toiled and have often gone without sleep; I have known hunger and thirst and have often gone without food; I have been cold and naked. Besides everything else, I face daily the pressure of my concern for all the churches. Who is weak, and I do not feel weak? Who is led into sin, and I do not inwardly burn? (11:23-29).

These painful trophies—labors for Christ, imprisonments, countless beatings, perils of frequent journeys, persecution by false brethren, poverty, and exposure to death—revealed Paul's greatness. The Corinthians had never heard a man extol his problems. That was a strange way to boast—the praise of hardships and suffering in ministry. The apostle explained: "If I must boast, I will boast of the things that show my weakness." A crowning example of the weakness and humiliation was his escape from Damascus (Acts 9:23-25). The Jews in the city were seeking to seize Paul. It appeared that he had no way of escape since the gates to the city were guarded. He did escape but not like a conquering hero. He was secretly let down by men—not angels—in a basket from a window in the city wall. Under those conditions he was helpless. How humiliating the experience would have been for his proud opponents. That kind of experience would have given them nothing about which to boast. But Paul preferred to call attention to God's grace and deliverance rather than to take ego trips.

All of Paul's values had been transformed by God's mighty work of reconciliation through the cross. The Corinthian rivals knew little, if anything, about God's renewing grace in Christ. They gloried in their triumphs. Paul gloried in humiliation. They gloried in popularity and applause. He gloried in honesty, sincerity, and God's approval. They gloried in pomp and power. Paul gloried in weakness. His weakness was like the "weakness of God" shown in the cross. It was "stronger than man's strength" (1 Cor. 1:25). The weakness manifested in the cross accomplished what human power had failed to achieve, that is, the healing of man's brokenness and his restoration to fellowship with God. That can be seen only by the eyes of faith.

The apostle's life was linked to Jesus Christ who enabled him to live triumphantly in the midst of great adversities. The same Christ who sustained Paul, is with the weak and tempted Christian. In fact He is with us in all our trials.

VI. CONCLUSION

As a servant of Christ Paul had the responsibility for the safe-guarding and advancing of faith and order. Daily the care of all the churches pressed upon Him (11:28). However, his ministry was fundamentally the same as that which belongs to every Christian—the ministry of reconciliation. The work of the ministry is a spiritual warfare with spiritual enemies. The weapons with which Christians are to wage war are the power of truth and the meekness of wisdom. These are mighty through God—no matter how feeble they appear to some. An antagonistic spirit, superior attitude, and self-righteousness do not attract people to the gospel and build up the church. A mature servant of Christ is by no means timid or lacking courage, but he proceeds with gentleness because his concern is for those whom he serves.

Spiritual problems cannot be solved by carnal means. Divine truth revealed in the Scriptures must be spoken in love. The peace of the church is an important matter, but it is not to be peace at any cost. Those who proclaim "a different Jesus" from the one of the New Testament have broken the unity of faith. Jude urges us "to contend for the faith that was once for all entrusted to the saints" (v. 3). Though we are not to be contentious, we are, as Paul did at Corinth, to contend for the faith. He knew, as we should, that reconciliation at the expense of truth is a false reconciliation. The downgrading of fundamental doctrine and the importance of biblical and theological soundness are signs of spiritual decadence. Changes that threaten the foundations of the church must be resisted. The church jeopardizes its own existence and betrays its Lord by accommodating error.

A group intruded and interferred in the church at Corinth by the means of doctrinal aberrations. Those people thought themselves to be spiritual superstars of that time, but they were false apostles who preached "a different Jesus." What we see in the modern type of free-lance evangelists and preachers whose efforts are devoted to gaining a following for themselves is not unknown in the New Testament. They work outside of the fellowship of the church; and like Paul's opponents, sometimes are antagonistic to the church and often make no effort to lead men and women into the continuing life of the church. As in the first century, evangelism must arise out of the heart of the church; it demands firm commitment to the fundamentals of the gospel and to the church.

However, the church needs a sense of balance. Christ and His gospel must not be compromised, but we must be open to the Holy Spirit and seek to understand each other whenever we differ on vital questions of faith or on other concerns. Through practicing together the ministry of reconciliation, we can conquer all conflicts and at the same time preserve the integrity of the gospel.

11

A Ministry of Grace and Power

2 Corinthians 12:1—13:14

God's final and most promising word to Paul was "My grace is sufficient for you, for my power is made perfect in weakness" (12:9). Divine grace worked in him and through his ministry, but God's power did not set him free from weakness of the thorn in the flesh, of life's perplexing problems, of frustration and hurts. As he lived his life in Christ and practiced the ministry of liberating reconciliation, he realized that God's grace was sufficient.

All Paul's Christian life and service depended on the divine grace and power. He spoke frequently and widely about grace in 2 Corinthians (1:2, 12; 4:15; 8:1,7,9; 9:8, 14). Basically, grace—undeserved favor—is the outpouring of God Himself in Christ and Christ's outpouring of Himself through the Holy Spirit. It is by grace that a man becomes a Christian and a minister of reconciliation.

Only by the means of divine favor was Paul made a servant in the church and in world-wide mission. The power of the Lord's all-sufficient grace was what made the apostle's constant suffering and hardships tolerable and enabled him to continue his work. When he was weak—despised, humiliated, poor, scorned by the world, and misunderstood by his spiritual children—he found strength. His human weakness set the best possible stage for the manifestation of God's mighty power. "The greater the servant's weakness, the more conspicuous is the power of his Master's all-sufficient grace."[1]

For Paul it was repugnant for a Christian to boast of his exploits. So if he must boast, he would boast only of his ministry in which he accepted weakness and found strength in grace to be more than adequate.

I. HIS VISIONS AND REVELATIONS (12:1-10)

The intruders at Corinth boasted of their special spiritual experiences in which the Lord appeared to them. Their claims impressed the Corinthians and made them wonder if Paul was an equal to the "super-spiritual" rivals. The whole business of boasting was distasteful to him, but now in the interest of the church he felt that he could not evade the question: "Had he had visionary experiences as they?" Though he had misgivings about what good would be served by sharing with them his most intimate and mysterious religious experiences,[2] he would do just that. Again, however, he would revert to the theme of weakness that magnified God's grace and power in his ministry.

A. An Experience in the Third Heaven (12:2-4)

Boasting about his "visions and revelations" was not to Paul's liking. Because of that he chose to veil his claim to visionary experience by referring to a third party—"a man in Christ." As verse 7 indicates, Paul was the "man in Christ." He recalled that "fourteen years ago" he had been caught up in the third heaven, the highest heaven, and that the experience was so magnificent that he did not know whether or not he was transported out of the body. This vision of God gave him knowledge that was inexpressible. The things that he was permitted to behold were so mysterious that human lips could not repeat them. Seeing the glories of the invisible world was a personal blessing and encouraged him in his difficult work, but these revelations were not to be told to others. Likely his opponents described in great detail what they saw and heard in their spiritual experiences, but Paul did not describe a single thing seen nor did he tell anything uttered. This might have been a rebuke to those at Corinth who cultivated mysterious spiritual experiences for public consumption.

---

[1] Philip E. Hughes, *Paul's Second Epistle to the Corinthians* (The New International Commentary on the New Testament), p. 451.

[2] That Paul did have visions and revelations is made clear in both Acts (16:9; 18:9; 22:17-18; 27:23) and Galatians (1:16; 2:2).

Being caught up into Paradise was a great privilege and was strength for ministry, but Paul refused to boast about it. He would boast only of his weaknesses. It was these—imprisonments, beatings, anxieties, and embarrassments (11:23-33)—that kept him from carnal pride and made him ready to receive God's grace and power, the only means by which he could effectively serve Christ. Should he have chosen to brag about his "visions and revelations" he would not have turned out to be a fool. Why? He would not have exaggerated but told only the truth about his spiritual experiences. It was likely that his rivals could not have in all honesty made that claim. They were spurred by the desire to be impressive and probably had boasted of religious experiences they had not had.

The apostle had no desire for false praise. Therefore he had deliberately refrained from boasting "so no one will think more of me than is warranted by what I do or say." He did not ask people to judge him by his secret visions but only by the life he lived and the message he proclaimed. If men's opinion of him had been too high, that would have obscured the fact that it was his message of reconciliation, not he himself, that they were to heed. He wanted to be understood and appreciated on the basis of his service. It is well for all servants of Christ to have the respect of those among whom they labor. Some have the respect of others because of their reputation for scholarship or spiritual gifts, but it can be sustained only by the life they live and the message they declare. A life consistent with the gospel will do more than anything to insure that people will continue to have confidence in us and give us a hearing.

B. An Experience of Pain (12:7-10)

After the apostle received "these surpassingly great revelations," he was sent the discipline of a thorn in the flesh. He had been caught up to Paradise. What he had seen and heard was too wonderful for utterance, but the next phase of his experience was with pain, which, except for the grace of God, would have been too much to bear.

1. His "thorn in the flesh" (12:7). Knowledge, particularly of the mysteries of God, could easily puff up a man. Paul could have been tempted to have unchristian pride in his visions. To keep him from becoming conceited he was given what he called "the thorn in the flesh." The word *thorn* (*skolops*) can be translated "stake," which was used for torture and execution. Exactly what the thorn in the flesh was we cannot be certain, but it was some kind of an ailment,[3] a stake that was sticking in his flesh. He described it as "a messenger of Satan," suggesting, therefore, that the ailment had come through a satanic messenger.

Whatever it was, "the thorn in the flesh" was for the purpose of keeping Paul's many visions and extraordinary experiences from going to his head. He was constantly tormented[4] by the thorn, and it made the daily discharge of his ministerial duties more difficult. The habitual drain of the painful discipline taught him humility. It reminded him that he was a man of like passion with those to whom he preached and made him depend on the grace and power of God. Thorns of life in our own flesh serve the same purpose. They are conducive to humility and Christian service, but spiritual pride is always fatal to usefulness in the Lord's work.

2. His prayer for deliverance (12:8-9a). The thorn really hurt. Smarting from the pain, the apostle prayed earnestly to be relieved of his trouble. Three times he begged God to set him free from it. The Lord said, "My grace is sufficient for you, for my power is made perfect in weakness." Christ did not give him a pre-packaged solution to his problem, or three steps through which he could overcome the weakness. He was assured of something better—the powerful grace of Christ. He was summoned by the Lord to accept his weakness and to find his strength in grace.

Grace can be stern. The Lord put aside Paul's prayer in which he pleaded and begged to be spared of any further pain of the thorn and told him: "My grace is all you need" (New English Bible). The grace that he received was sufficient to bear the pain and to endure the strain. His weakness did not hinder the effectiveness of God's power, but rather it provided the greatest opportunity for the display of divine power. "My power," as the Lord said, "is made perfect in weakness." The fact was, as Paul realized, that precisely where he was weak God could be strong. And that was better for the apostle and his ministry. God cannot help or use self-sufficient people but only those who have a deep dependence on Him. Where there is weakness and openness to

---

[3]Paul's "thorn in the flesh" has been variously identified as malaria, epilepsy, disease of the eyes, insomnia, or migraine headaches. The fact that he endured great perils and hardships indicates that generally his health was good. If the thorn is understood to have been a physical defect, it could have been a speech impediment. This could account for the charge of his being weak in presence and in speech but impressive through his letters (10:1, 9-11; 11:6). However, this is nothing more than a guess.

[4]The present subjunctive of *kolaphizō* ("torment," "buffet") implies that in his daily round of life and ministry he was tormented.

divine grace His mighty power comes clearly in view. As with the apostle, human inadequacy may be an occasion for the triumph of grace.

3. His submission to the Lord (12:9b-10).   The kind of bragging that Paul's rivals did was foolishness.[5] He wished to show that he could boast also, only in a different way. His was a strange sort of boasting, but it reflected submission to the Lord—"I will boast all the more gladly about my weaknesses." The divine answer to his prayer was that power would come, not by overcoming his weakness but by bearing it. Apparently some weaknesses are not to be overcome. Through them God's power is perfected.

The apostle did not take a fatalistic attitude toward his weaknesses, but he "more gladly" took delight in his troubles. When he accepted the Lord's answer, he was willing to settle for weaknesses. The fact is that he gloried in them, not because the endurance of pain was in itself virtuous but because they were the means of something greater. Here is a profound truth: Paul's weaknesses would end in power. He knew that Christ's power would rest on him as God's cloud of glory had rested on the Temple. That was why he took delight "in weaknesses, in insults, in hardships, in persecutions, in difficulties." These meant power, for as he said, "When I am weak [by human standards], then I am strong."

Nothing but his total reliance on God's powerful grace was Paul's boast. Christ did not ask him to become infantile and turn his back on all that he had learned from the hard experiences of life. It was not that God's grace denied him his own strength nor does it deny us our strength. The experience of Paul reminds us that human strength is not to be at the center of our lives. To rely on our strength is to implant our own self firmly at the center. All that God asks is that our weakness and strength be conformed to the likeness of Christ.

In serving Christ there are no guarantees of freedom from trouble. The Savior never promised us that. Paul, one of God's greatest servants, did not find it that way. It was when he was weak in his ministry, lacking physical and spiritual strength, that the power of God would work through him. The fact is that grace has always been and will always be enough—sufficient for the tasks that confront us.

---

[5] As a polemic against his opponents Paul called his own boasting foolishness (*aphrosunē*, 11:1,17,21; cf. *aphrōn*, 11:16,19; 12:11; but see 12:6).

II. HIS COMMENDATION AND TRUST (12:11-21)

The Corinthians had failed Paul. They had not defended him against the vicious attacks on his character and ministry. The truth was that they listened to his critics. Because his spiritual children did not take his side, he was forced in his own defense to commend himself. Against his better judgment he boasted. Therefore he admitted: "I have made a fool of myself." The commendation of the Corinthians would have spared him of such foolishness. Though they did not take his side, he was confident that because of the grace and power of God in no way was he inferior to the "super-apostles." He was really superior.

A. Marks of an Apostle (12:12)

The opponents had claimed miracles, that is, the very marks of a true apostle. These were described by Paul as "signs, wonders and miracles." It would be a mistake to sharply distinguish these one from another. *Signs* are events which are seen to have spiritual significance and to reveal the grace of God at work. *Wonders* are happenings that are astounding and extraordinary in character. *Miracles* stress the power of God at work and are seen especially in physical healings.

All these had marked Paul's ministry at Corinth. The spiritual gifts operated through him and mighty deeds accompanied his ministry. No claim was made by him to have performed miracles, but rather he said that they "were done among you" by the power of God.[6] Healings and other supernatural signs confirmed his ministry. Though the charismatic gifts worked through his ministry, the Holy Spirit did not exempt him from suffering. Apparently, unlike his opponents, he never let the ministry of miracles get out of focus. He recognized, as we should, that many gifts other than healing are needed—faith, wisdom, knowledge, teaching, generosity, prophecy (Rom. 12:6-8, 1 Cor. 12:8-10; Eph. 4:11).

Spiritual gifts are for the whole community of faith. They are not restricted to exceptional individuals or super-charismatic personalities. Some people have made grandiose claims in regard to the gifts of the Spirit, but the gifts are not for the purpose of exalting those through whom they operate. When a

---

[6]The passive "were done" (*kateirgasthē*) credits the mighty works to God. See also Romans 15:18-19. The phrase "with great perseverance" implies that the miraculous signs were wrought under hardships that required endurance in the prosecution of the ministry.

man lays his hands on us in prayer, there is no power in those hands. They are flesh and no more, but God may minister to us through him.

The biblical view of gifts is that they are manifestations of God's grace and power and have a servant role. Gifts are bestowed on Christians so that they may serve others and build up the church.

B. Freedom from Greed (12:13-18)

The Corinthian Christians had been treated the same as all the other churches, with one exception: Paul had not been a financial burden to them. In their midst miracles had been performed, but they felt "inferior" (*hēssōthēte*, "you were put lower") to the other churches because Paul had refused to take support from them. That was no sign that he thought less of them, but apparently they were offended because of it. He wanted to be reconciled to the church. Therefore with some irony he said, "Forgive me this wrong!" If that were a barrier between them, he wanted their forgiveness so that their fellowship could be restored. The apostle was interested in their spiritual welfare, not in their money.

1. His interest was unselfish (12:14).   For a third time Paul planned to visit Corinth. On his forthcoming visit he would make no change in his financial policy. He still would not be a burden to the church. For he wanted the Corinthians, not their possessions. He desired to cultivate and maintain warm fellowship with them and to see them committed fully to Jesus Christ. He had begotten the Corinthians as Christians. As their spiritual father, he did not expect material returns for nurturing his children. His financial policy was justified by a simple analogy from human life: Children are not expected to provide for the future security of their parents but parents for their children. The basic necessities—food, clothing, and shelter—are not normally provided by children. Parents have the responsibility for providing these. The apostle was prepared to accept his full responsibility for his children in the faith. More than anything he desired to see them give wholehearted devotion to Christ.

2. He planned to spend himself for their spiritual good (12:15).   Time, energy, and love Paul had, but he had little else. Gladly he would be spent and would spend what he had for his beloved children. The verb *spend* (*dapanaō*) refers to Paul's manual labor to support himself and his ministry. He was ready to spend himself completely and labor untiringly in their behalf. No matter the cost, he was eager to help the Corinthians.

What disturbed him was their ungratefulness. He had lavished his affection on the Corinthians. Ordinarily love kindles love. It was most unnatural for them to lessen their love for Paul since he would spare no effort to serve them. The influence of the intruders seems to have cooled their affection for him. Less love on their part did not stop him from loving them just as parents go on loving their rebellious children. He did not bluntly condemn them. He left the way open for his ungrateful children to change their attitude and to meet him with love.

3. *He did not take advantage of them (12:16-19).* That Paul had not been a burden was undeniable. Though he had not asked for money for himself, he had been a "crafty fellow," his adversaries said, using Titus and others to get money from Corinth and thus took them "by trickery" (*dolōi,* "guile," "deceit"). This attack was directed against the raising of the collection for the poor Christians in Jerusalem. The charge was dismissed. He had not exploited (*pleonekteō,* "take advantage") them through Titus and the unnamed Christian brothers. These men were honest and made nothing out of the church. Paul, too, had precisely the same spirit of integrity and acted in the same way.

The apostle had defended himself against the charges of the "super-apostles." The saving of his reputation, however, was not his concern. What he had said was spoken "in the sight of God." His case had been argued, not so much before the Corinthians, but before the judgment bar of God. It was God's standards that he would have to satisfy. If he were not seeking to justify himself in their eyes, why did he bother to speak? His reply was: "Everything we do, dear friends, is for your strengthening" (*oikodomēs,* "building up"). His aim was to clear away the obstacles erected by the trouble makers to hinder Christian fellowship and to create a climate in which differences could be resolved. His controlling desire was for reconciliation, a relationship rooted in God's grace and characterized by mutual love and trust.

C. Apprehension About the Spiritual Condition of the Church (12:20-21)[7]

When Titus brought him news of the Corinthians' repentance, Paul was more than pleased (7:9-16). Despite his joy, he was not going to overlook what could

---

[7]In chapters 10-13 Paul's firmness is due to the intruders and their disrupting influence on the church. As we have already noted, Paul had been concerned that he might have been too harsh in the "severe letter" that he wrote out of love for the Corinthians (2:4; 7:8); but Titus brought him encouraging news that they had repented. Mutual confidence and fellowship were restored between Paul and his converts. There were, however, intruders who sought to seduce his spiritual

prove to be detrimental to the church. Reconciliation required alertness to spiritual dangers. There were still some problems which made Paul concerned about what might become of the church. When he visited Corinth again, he warned that they might find his words far from pleasant. Should he find that some had not abandoned the "works of the flesh," they would not find him to their liking. He would have to exercise his authority and deal sternly with sin. On his next visit he was afraid that he would discover two things.

1. He feared finding divisiveness in the church (12:20).   The intrusion of the rival apostles was disruptive to the Christian fellowship. Paul listed eight sins that he dreaded to find: "quarreling, jealousy, outbursts of anger, factions, slander, gossip, arrogance and disorder." This catalogue consists of spiritual sins which frequently do not appear sinful to those who are involved in them. These sins are not the flagrant sins of vice and sexual immorality but of carnal disposition. These destroy the peace of the church. These are divisive and cause schisms in the body of Christ.

2. He feared being humiliated[8] before them (12:21).   Paul had had moments of humiliation. He had been grieved by the unfaithfulness that he had found at Corinth (2:1; 7:12). He feared another unpleasant experience like that. If he found on his third visit that some were unrepentant of sins of impurity, he would be humbled again. That would have been defeat for him. His rivals could boast that he could not get his converts to mend their ways and live righteously. He feared this humiliation. The reason was that the strengthening of the church meant everything to him. Through his own strength Paul could not build up the church. He himself had weaknesses, but he was a minister of reconciliation in whom the all-powerful Lord dwelt. Thus there was power in weakness.

---

children from the pure gospel. This explains Paul's firmness, especially in chapters 12 and 13. What he states in these chapters should not be viewed as being a contradiction to full and complete reconciliation reflected in chapter 7. His loving concern for his converts impelled him to warn them of the dangers of the false apostles who preached "a different Jesus" and "a different gospel." Paul did not condemn the whole church, but that element in the church that was undermining the faith and destroying the fellowship of the true believers. He reminded the Corinthians: "Everything we do, dear friends, is for your strengthening" (12:19).

[8]The New International Version renders the verb *tapeinoō* as "humble," but often it means "humiliate" and seems to have that nuance here.

III. HIS POWER AND AUTHORITY (13:1-9)

The "super-apostles" had created a divisive spirit in the church. Paul knew that and, too, that there was the danger of moral disorder. Should that be the circumstances that existed on his third visit, he would deal sternly with the offenders. Of course he preferred to exercise his authority by love rather than by power, but he would take disciplinary action if it was necessary.

A. His Warning (13:1-2)

Upon coming again, he would deal sternly with those guilty of moral laxity and of contention and strife. First, he would execute justice. According to the Mosaic law no one could be condemned on the evidence of one witness (Deut. 19:15). There had to be two or more corroborating witnesses before a charge could be considered proven. The apostle would not hesitate to execute justice, but it would be carried out in accord with the Old Testament principle: "Every matter must be established by the testimony of two or three witnesses."

Second, he would not spare the sinner. The time of forebearance was past. On the immoral and the troublemakers who refused to repent, penalties would be imposed. He hoped that this warning would lead them to change; but as a last resort, he was prepared to exclude them from the church (cf. 1 Cor. 5:1-5).

B. His Authority (13:3-4)

With typical directness Paul made clear that he would not spare the obstinate and unrepentant. By their own deeds they had alienated themselves from the grace of God. His rivals demanded proof that Christ was speaking through the apostle. They insisted that they saw no evidence of the power of Christ at work in Paul. The apostle would not accommodate them by offering them some striking evidence of his authority and spirituality.

Paul's opponents did not understand that in weakness God's power is perfectly revealed. He saw himself as weak but strong through God (12:9-10; 4:7; 10-12). The weakness and power in the experience of Paul was paralleled in Jesus Christ. On the cross Christ appeared as only a helpless man, and He died in weakness. Through that weakness was released God's power that triumphed over death and that provided the ground for reconciliation. Christ's resurrection and life showed His divine power. Crucified in His weakness, "he lives by God's power." So no matter how contemptible and weak

172

Paul appeared to the world, yet as a servant of Christ he manifested the power and authority of God. He was confident that God would grant him sufficient strength to deal with the situation at Corinth.[9] The power of the risen Christ would enable him to deal decisively and effectively with the dissidents and the immoral. His desire was to build up the church, not to destroy it.

C. His Call for Self-Examination (13:5-9)

The troublemakers at Corinth had been testing the wrong person. They had insisted that Paul present evidence of his authority, but they were to test themselves, not Paul. They had kept looking for faults in him and had doubted the purity of his motives and demanded proof of his power, but it was their position in Christ that was suspect. Three times he challenged them and us—"Examine yourselves...test yourselves...realize that Christ is in you."

1. The purpose of the test—"whether you are in the faith" (13:5). They had wanted him to offer a sensational proof of his authority. Now he challenged them to look at themselves. To them he submitted one test: Were they in the faith? Could they show evidence of their salvation and sanctification? They were to give what assurance they could that they were saved and not lost. There was doubt that some of them were really Christians. Believers can test their faith. There are the measuring instruments of the Holy Spirit and the Word of God. Besides these are purity of life, kindness, love, good works, worship, and others.

2. The possible results of the test—"that we have not failed the test" (13:6-9). Through Paul's ministry the Corinthians became Christians. He hoped that before he arrived in Corinth those who had doubts about his authority would realize that he was a true minister of Christ. If they realized this, they would repent and work at restoring Christian fellowship among them. Therefore they would become zealous of spiritual improvement, and he would not have to deal with strife and sin in the church. That would make it unnecessary for Paul to be severe with them.

   The apostle prayed for reformation. He prayed that every church member would act rightly, even if he failed the test. He could not work against the truth but only for it. His desire was for the truth of the gospel to prevail. To it his

---

[9]This is implied by Paul's statement in verse 4: "By God's power we will live with him to serve you."

whole life was committed. His ministry of reconciliation, as he had often said, involved his weakness. But he was glad when they were morally and spiritually strong, though he was weak. His prayer was for their perfection (*katartisis*, "restoration"). A number of the Corinthians needed to bring themselves in line with the gospel so they could be restored to the Christian life.

IV. CLOSING APPEAL (13:10-14)

Away from Corinth Paul had written as he had, so that he would not have to discipline some in the church. God had given him authority to build up but not to destroy them. However he used the divinely conferred authority, even if he had to take drastic action to restore them to the Christian life, it would be in accord with the Lord's will. The real work of the ministry is always constructive. Its aim is the building of Christian fellowship.

A. Final Exhortations (13:11-12)

As Paul brought the letter to a close, he struck a note of encouragement and urged the readers to mend their ways and live in harmony.

His last appeal to them was fourfold. First, "Aim for perfection"—literally, "Pull yourselves together." This called for reformation among them and continuous growth in grace. The challenge was for them to restore the broken relationships that still existed among them. The divisive parties were to become one and live in harmony.

Second, "Listen to one another."[10] They were to keep on encouraging one another and engage in a mutual ministry of exhorting one another to pursue the Christian life.

Third, "Be of one mind." Divisive tendencies were common at Corinth. They were urged to be willing to agree with one another and assume responsibility for creating harmony.

Fourth, "Live in peace." Living in harmony required the continuous process of reconciliation. If they would do these things, Paul assured them that "the God of love and peace" would be with them. "The peace of God" here is recon-

---

[10]The New International Version renders *parakaleisthe* "listen to my appeal," but it can be understood to be in the middle voice and therefore is better translated "listen to one another" or "exhort one another."

ciliation which is through the divine gift of grace and issues into restoration of fellowship with God and with one another.

B. Benediction (13:14)

The very heart of reconciliation is grace, love, and fellowship, all of which Paul included in the benediction. "The grace of the Lord Jesus Christ" has opened the way to reconciliation with God and man. "The love of God" reached out through Christ to put an end to man's estrangement and to restore him to fellowship with God. "The fellowship of the Holy Spirit" is the fellowship which the Holy Spirit calls into being within the church. The Holy Spirit, who is the Spirit of love and fellowship, creates a community of reconciliation that crosses all frontiers of race, class, and other human divisions and that embraces those who are similar and dissimilar.

V. CONCLUSION

Committed to the gospel, the apostle Paul by divine authority proclaimed and defended the message "that God was reconciling the world to himself in Christ" (5:19). He was consumed by the ministry of reconciliation, which indeed is a ministry of grace and power. The pivot of the ministry of reconciliation is Jesus Christ and His cross. "When the time had fully come, God sent his Son" (Gal. 4:4). The Old Testament discloses that God sought to enter into fellowship with man in earlier historical periods, but His reconciling work moved out into the open and took a decisive leap forward in Jesus Christ. The ministry of reconciliation was accomplished by Christ.

God has transferred this ministry to us all. Everyone who calls himself a Christian is intended to be a reconciler. Jesus' ministry was to break down the partitions that separated men from God and from one another and that He did, but the ministry of reconciliation is a continuing task. Many are still unreconciled. They need to hear the invitation to a new and fulfilling relationship, offered as a gift of grace from God in Christ.

What is so tragic is that the barriers to great spiritual accomplishments are often so petty. Many local congregations are immobilized because of personality conflicts, and this says nothing about serious disagreements among churchmen in high places which stymie whole denominations. There is no doubt that the line between creative diversity and destructive divisions in the church is difficult to draw with precision; but the problem of a strife-torn church is nothing more than the problem of sin and reflects the poverty of the relation of the members to Christ.

No child of God has any basis for complacency. Every Christian needs to strive to build up the church and to make manifest its unity. However, the fulness of reconciliation must wait until the Last Day when everything is put in subjection to Jesus Christ, "so that God may be all in all" (1 Cor. 15:28). That will bring the ultimate triumph of reconciliation. Alienation, estrangement, conflict, meaninglessness, and despair will find no place in the final reign of God. The broken world will be transformed in the coming kingdom and complete justice, true freedom, unlimited love, and everlasting peace will be realized. "People will come from east and west and north and south, and will take their places at the feast in the kingdom of God" (Luke 13:29). "The creation itself will be liberated from its bondage to decay and brought into the glorious freedom of the children of God" (Rom. 8:21).

Bibliography

Arrington, French L. *Divine Order in the Church*. Cleveland, Tennessee: Pathway Press, 1978.

——————. *Paul's Aeon Theology in I Corinthians*. Washington, D.C.: University Press of America, 1977.

Bailey, J. Martin. *From Wrecks to Reconciliation*. New York: Friendship Press, 1969.

Barclay, William. *The Letters to the Corinthians*. Philadelphia: Westminster Press, 1956.

Barrett, Charles Kingsley. *A Commentary on the Second Epistle to the Corinthians*. Harper's New Testament Commentaries. New York: Harper and Row, 1973.

Bauer, Walter, William F. Arndt and F. Wilbur Gingrich. *A Greek English Lexicon of the New Testament and Other Early Christian Literature*. Chicago: University of Chicago Press, 1961.

Beach, Waldo. *The Christian Life*. Atlanta: John Knox Press, 1967.

Blass, Friedrick and Albert Debrunner. *A Greek Grammar of the New Testament and Other Early Christian Literature*. Translated and revised by Robert W. Funk. Chicago: University of Chicago Press, 1961.

Bornkamm, Günther. *Paul*. Translated by D.M.G. Stalker. New York: Harper and Row, 1971.

Bromiley, G.W. *Christian Ministry*. Grand Rapids, Michigan: William B. Eerdmans Publishing Co., 1959.

Bruce, Frederick Fyvie. *Paul, Apostle of the Heart Set Free*. Grand Rapids: William B. Eerdmans Publishing Co., 1977.

Come, Arnold B. *Agents of Reconciliation*. Philadelphia: Westminster Press, 1964.

Cullmann, Oscar. *The Early Church*. Translated by A.J.B. Higgins and Stanley Godman. Philadelphia: Westminster Press, 1966.

Denney, James. *The Christian Doctrine of Reconciliation*. New York: George H. Doran, 1918.

Ditmanson, Harold H. *Grace in Experience and Theology*. Minneapolis: Augsburg Publishing House, 1977.

BIBLIOGRAPHY

Filson, Floyd V. and James Reid. *The Second Epistle to the Corinthians.* The Interpreter's Bible. New York: Abingdon-Cokesbury Press, 1953.

Fisher, Robert E. *The Family and the Church.* Cleveland, Tennessee: Pathway Press, 1978.

Gale, Herbert M. *The Use of Analogy in the Letters of Paul.* Philadelphia: Westminster Press, 1964.

Gray, James Comper and George M. Adams. *Gray and Adams Bible Commentary.* Grand Rapids: Zondervan, n.d.

Hughes, Philip E. *The Second Epistle to the Corinthians.* The New International Commentary on the New Testament. Grand Rapids: William B. Eerdmans Publishing Co., 1962.

Hunter, Archibald. *Probing the New Testament.* Richmond: John Knox Press, 1972.

Inch, Morris A. *My Servant Job.* Grand Rapids: Baker Book House, 1979.

Künneth, Walter. *The Theology of the Resurrection.* St. Louis: Concordia Publishing House, 1965.

Kwiran, Manfred. *The Resurrection of the Dead.* Basel: Friedrick Reinhardt Kommissionserlag, 1972.

Lenski, R.C.H. *Interpretation of First and Second Corinthians.* Minneapolis: Augsburg, 1935.

Martin, Ralph P. *New Testament Foundations: A Guide for Christian Students.* Grand Rapids: William B. Eerdmans Publishing Co., 1975.

Munck, Johannes. *Paul and the Salvation of Mankind.* Translated by Frank Clark. Richmond: John Knox Press, 1959.

Nickle, Keith F. *The Collection.* Naperville, Illinois: A.R. Allenson, 1966.

Roetzel, Calvin J. *Judgment in the Community.* Leiden: E.J. Brill, 1972.

Scroggie, W. Graham. *Know Your Bible.* London: Pickering & Inglis Ltd., 1965.

Strachan, R.H. *The Second Epistle of Paul to the Corinthians.* Moffatt New Testament Commentaries. New York: Harper and Brothers, n.d.

Whitley, D.E.H. *The Theology of St. Paul.* Philadelphia: Fortress Press, 1972.

8955